Underwater Hunting

Its Techniques and Adventures

Bill Barada

Underwater Hunting
Its Techniques and Adventures

Introduction by Paul J. Tzimoulis

Doubleday & Company, Inc.
Garden City, New York 1969

Also by Bill Barada

WORLD BENEATH THE SEA
Contributor
LET'S GO DIVING
MASK AND FLIPPERS
with Lloyd Bridges
ADVENTURE UNDERWATER
UNDERWATER

Library of Congress Catalog Card Number 69–15206

Acknowledgments

I am keenly aware of my debt to those thousands of unnamed pioneers of skin diving who have shared their hard-won knowledge, skills and techniques to make the writing of this book possible. Many of these are diving buddies; others I have consulted personally or by mail and phone. It is impossible to thank all of these people by name, but a few deserve special mention. To my wife, Harriet, for her encouragement, criticism and editing assistance I owe a private gratitude. To the Atlantis Divers Club members for their unique contribution to this book I extend a specific thanks. To Dewey Bergman, Allan Boehm, Jim Brown, John Hoynacki, Terry Maas, H. Gene Martin, Ron Merker, Dan Nelson, Martin Pasos, Farley Sonnier, Burr Tettleton, Jerry Turner, Bob White, Omar Wood, Frank Xedus, Ann Frame, and the photographers whose names appear with the pictures, my sincere appreciation for providing special information and material.

Contents

Regional, national and world champions of underwater spearfishing
. . . Amateur Athletic Union competition sponsored by the Underwater Society of America and the World Confederation (CMAS) . . .
The rigorous training and endurance required . . . Amazing feats are
routine for a champion.

Introduction

ONE of the most primitive and strongest of man's instincts is the desire to hunt. It is an inner force rooted deep within the very chromosomes of our make-up. Primeval man stalked mastodons with stone and club, so that his tribe might survive the rigors of a crude world.

Today, the necessity to hunt for food has given way to sport and recreation. Since he cannot rid himself of this prehistoric urge, man now has learned how to channel his instinctive desire into a rewarding, civilized effort. It seems that Americans are especially proud of their hunting prowess, and evidence of this can be noted in the fact that we have 18 million registered hunters. Each year, this hardy group of outdoor enthusiasts tracks America's uplands and swamps in search of game or wild fowl—enjoying the natural heritage of their pioneering forefathers.

It is only fitting a book about underwater hunting be written, thus opening a door to new hunting grounds. Beneath the surface lies a whole new frontier, containing far more game than all the lands of all the continents. It is the last frontier left on this planet, still full of mystery, adventure and discovery. What better challenge for man's skill and instinct?

It is also fitting that the author of this guide to underwater hunting be Bill Barada, America's oldest, most experienced underwater hunter. He is a legend within his own time—a veritable Daniel Boone of the undersea world.

Bill made his first underwater spear in 1935, and hunted game in the chilly waters off the Southern California coast. Since that first narcotic plunge, he has traveled around the world—mastering all known forms of underwater hunting and testing every contrived contraption for taking marine game. His quest has led Bill to octopus ridge in Puget Sound, the shark infested seas of French Polynesia, the offshore-oil rigs of the Gulf of Mexico, the Great Lakes, the East Coast, the West Coast, the Caribbean, Mexico, and a dozen more equally fascinating waters. No other diver has roamed so far, and hunted so keenly as Bill Barada.

Underwater Hunting fills a vital gap in diver education, for it is the first comprehensive work on this subject. Every scuba-class graduate will want to have a copy, so that he may continue learning the special skills necessary for successful adaptation to this liquid environment. It is not enough to be taught the basic fundamentals of scuba and skin diving. One must know how to *apply* these new-found tools, as well as handle them safely. Bill Barada has done a superb job of supplying the knowledge, know-how and fish sense for good hunting techniques.

Most neophytes take "underwater hunting" to mean the stalking and shooting of fish. In this remarkably broad book, Bill Barada has added chapter after chapter on other forms of hunting. Abalone, clams, conch and live marine tropicals are treated with equal importance. There is a whole chapter devoted to lobster and octopus, and another on hunting with a camera in place of the spear gun. *Underwater Hunting* can serve as a valuable handbook for just about anyone who is planning to explore the undersea world.

Read it carefully . . . happy hunting!

Paul J. Tzimoulis
Editor & Publisher
SKIN DIVER MAGAZINE

Underwater Hunting

Its Techniques and Adventures

A hunter descending into an offshore reef never knows what game lies hidden in the depths. (*Photo by Paul Tzimoulis*)

1 Hunting vs. Sightseeing

SLIPPING beneath the surface off Catalina Island, I hung suspended in mid-water. For a few moments I enjoyed the tranquillity and solitude of being alone in the sea, and felt the exhilarating sensation of weightlessness and freedom experienced only when scuba diving. The clear blue water of the Pacific revealed a seascape of breathtaking beauty. Below me was a submarine canyon, its walls a craggy jumble of sharp pinnacles and projections that plunged downward into the depths. Covering the bottom, clinging to the rocks and filling every crevice, a dark-green jungle of vegetation softened the harshness of the reef. Beneath its protective shadows, slight movements and flashes of silver indicated the presence of fish hiding in the darkness. Around me was a forest of giant kelp, its long strands intertwined into great trunks that swept upward from the bottom in graceful arcs to float its leaves in the sunlight on the surface. Schools of brightly colored fish flitted in and out of its branches like a flight of birds on the wing.

The entire scene swayed to and fro in the undulating rhythm of passing swells.

At times like these I feel sorry for those poor land-bound souls who
have never seen the brilliant beauty of a tropical coral reef, or experienced the sensation of "flying" over a submerged mountain range,
or drifted slowly over the ripples and undulations of a great undersea
desert. Not long ago the watery world beneath the surface was considered a mysterious and dangerous place, inhabited by voracious sea
monsters waiting to attack any hapless swimmer who ventured into
their domain. These are fears and apprehensions handed down from
a superstitious past. Modern scuba divers have discovered this concept to be pure nonsense. The skin diver's face mask is a magic win-
dow through which the underwater world is revealed as a strange and
beautiful place inhabited by exotic and friendly creatures. Swimming
into this world is like swimming into a paradise. The first few times
you go underwater you feel a little like Alice in Wonderland. And
every time you dive this feeling of fantasy returns. It is a fluid world of
wildly beautiful surroundings where nothing is familiar. The terrain
is always below you, and you must learn to move like a fish, gliding
and swimming above it rather than walking on firm ground. But,
once you have mastered your equipment and become accustomed to
the environment, the possibilities for excitement and adventure are
as limitless as the oceans themselves.

Three quarters of the earth is covered by water, and the submarine
terrain offers a variety of seascapes every bit as spectacular as anything on land. Its great, sandy deserts are so huge they make the Sa-
hara seem like a neighborhood sandlot in comparison. Submerged
mountains, with their tips brushing the surface and their bases in the
abyssal depths, are so tall that, if placed side by side, they would
dwarf the highest peak on land. Great oceanic rivers circle the continents from the poles to the tropics, their currents distributing the
water like giant thermostats which determine and control the weather
of the earth. The inhabitants of the oceans range in size from microscopic plankton, which are the smallest animals on earth, to the great
sperm whales, which are the largest mammals known. Between these
two extremes is such a dazzling array of animal and plant life that it
staggers the imagination, and scientists are discovering new varie-

ties almost every day. The vast majority of these marine animals are found in the shallow water bordering the shore. Here, in depths of less than 200 feet, sunlight penetrates the water with life-giving rays to spark the food chain of the sea. It is the spawning ground and hatchery for myriads of mollusks, crustaceans and fish of all sizes, shapes and colors which find refuge among the rocks, coral, seaweed and sand of the inshore reefs. This is the hunting ground of the predators, the great game fish and mammals of the open sea who prowl the coasts in search of food. It is also the hunting ground of the skin diver; a place of fantastic beauty in which you can swim over rocky reefs, where every square inch is covered with colorful, clinging marine animals, their delicate shapes and slender tendrils appearing like flowers in a marine garden. Here you can hang suspended along the sheer faces of underwater precipices, drift over bottomless submarine canyons, or cruise past jagged reefs with crevices and caves draped by clinging kelp and seaweed. In clear, tropical waters, such as the Car-

At times like these I feel sorry for those poor land-bound souls who have never experienced the sensation of flying through a submarine forest. (*Photo by Chuck Nicklin, The Diving Locker*)

The shallow water of inshore reefs is a prolific hunting ground for skin divers. Even the casual observer will see fantastic sights and encounter game in unbelievable abundance. (*Photo by Paul Tzimoulis*)

ibbean, you will see spectacular gardens and entire islands of living coral, whose beautifully grotesque shapes and gaudy colors appear as if painted by an artist gone mad. And through it all, along every shoreline of the world, is a panorama of moving, changing sea life. Schools of small fish dart and weave through open water. Brilliantly hued reef fish form a kaleidoscope of moving color around bizarre coral heads. Every crack, crevice and cave is occupied by a colony of sea creatures. Here also are the sea denizens. Moving through open water, prowling the bottom, or hiding deep in underwater caves, are the animals sought by underwater hunters. They may be choice specimens weighing only a few pounds or giants ten times the size of a man. It is truly another world, the last unexplored frontier and the greatest hunting grounds on earth. Even the casual observer will see fantastic sights and encounter game in unbelievable abundance. Even the novice hunter will find a few species that he can successfully capture. But, just as in the mountains, forests and jungles on land, most of the choice sea creatures are past masters at camouflage, are very alert to danger, and it requires the knowledge, skill and trained eye of an underwater hunter to detect them. In the underwater world, as on the surface, there is a great difference between hunting and sightseeing and many of the most exciting creatures and choice game are never seen by the novice or the casual observer.

I will never forget my first dive into the waters of the Pacific off the Palos Verdes Peninsula in Southern California. It was in 1935 and my equipment consisted of a pair of homemade goggles, and a hand spear made from a broom handle. I plunged into the water at Malaga Cove, fully expecting to see the bottom crawling with lobsters and shellfish, and the water swarming with fish which would accommodate me by posing quietly in front of my crude weapon. I was totally unprepared for the sight my goggles revealed. It was like nothing I had ever seen before. I floated above a jagged, rocky reef, its walls broken and slashed with deep cavities and clefts which led downward into dimness and shadows. Its surface was covered with a jungle of blue and purple marine vegetation which waved to and fro as if pushed by a constantly changing wind. Sunlight filtering through the dense foliage created moving patches of light and shadow through which I caught glimpses of red, orange and yellow growths tucked beneath the canopy of green. A few small bait fish darted in and out of the kelp, and I could see mussels, barnacles, sea urchins and other organisms clinging to the rocks. But the schools of food fish and colonies of lobsters which I had expected were nowhere to be seen. I swam and dived for half an hour looking for a target. The largest fish I saw was a brilliantly colored garibaldi, or Catalina goldfish, which stood out among the dark foliage like a neon sign. Even this brazen hussy eluded my clumsy efforts and I came ashore empty handed, convinced that the area I had selected was a barren ocean and the game fish must be living somewhere else. Years later, after I had gained considerable experience, I learned that this first spot was one of the most productive hunting grounds along the coast.

That was more than thirty years ago, but today, even with modern scuba equipment and sophisticated weapons, my first experience is being repeated over and over again throughout the world. An example occurred recently while Clint Harte, another old-timer, and I were sitting on the rocks in the same spot at Palos Verdes. Two young skin divers came out of the water, looked at our gear and advised, "You're wasting your time here. It's all fished out. We covered the whole area and there is nothing here."

We didn't say anything. Any comment we made would have embarrassed them and been resented. But we went out after they had gone and caught enough fish and lobsters to feed our families.

This type of experience is familiar to old-timers at underwater hunting. It isn't that hunters are better divers than those who prefer just to go sightseeing and exploring. Modern instruction classes which include open-water experience, and the many books on diving, can make almost anyone competent to handle himself and his equipment in the water. The difference between hunting and sightseeing is that the hunter has learned to penetrate the camouflage of sea creatures, knows their habits and where to find them, and has learned to approach within range of a spear gun. As a result, he sees more than the sightseeing diver ever will, and I believe his knowledge makes diving more rewarding even when he is not looking for game.

The casual observer will see the more curious and bolder specimens and he will be surrounded by young fry who haven't yet learned the caution that comes with age and experience. But the larger, more desirable game didn't grow to a ripe old age by being stupid or careless. The law of survival in the oceans is "eat or be eaten" just as it is in the jungle, and its wise inhabitants stay out of range or head for cover at any sign of danger. To hunt successfully, a skin diver must stalk his game with every bit as much skill and patience as a hunter on land with a rifle. He must learn the habits of his quarry, where its hiding places are, how to penetrate its camouflage, how to approach within range and, finally, how to catch it and bring it to the surface. Even choice shellfish, crabs and lobsters do not lie around on the bottom like so many rocks waiting to be picked up. These creatures are experts at deception, taking advantage of every kind of natural cover they can find or devise. Some shellfish and crustaceans dress themselves with barnacles and seaweed and, when lying quietly on the bottom, they look like any other rock. Many times I have put my hand next to what I thought was a seaweed-covered rock only to have it start up and scurry away over the sandy bottom. Close inspection disclosed my "rock" to be a sand-dwelling crab that deliberately drapes its body with seaweed to confuse its enemies. Others, such as the spiny lobsters, hide in cracks and holes, using their feelers as antennae to detect the presence of food or enemies. Many a diver has passed by a colony of lobsters, mistaking their projecting antennae for seaweed or coral. Rock-dwelling mollusks, such as abalone and rock scallops, are found nestled among sea urchins, barnacles, seaweed and other organisms growing on the rocks. Usually these shells are covered with marine growth and it takes a keen eye to spot them. I have watched divers pass by an abalone or rock scallop which was resting less than a foot in front of their face masks. There are tricks to recognizing this type of animal, which will be covered in a later chapter. But, although every area has its own species of game, with different habits and hiding places, once these tricks are mastered, they will help you spot similar game in almost any area.

The first time a group of us visited San Carlos Bay near Guaymas, Mexico, we had no knowledge of the waters of the Gulf of California and had no idea of what kind of marine life we could expect to find. We were hunting fish, but, out of long habit, I cruised close to the bottom, holding to the rocks and peering into holes and caves. I noticed some odd-shaped formations clinging to the rocks which were slightly different from their surroundings. At first glance they looked like a part of the rock, but what caught my eye was that these particular clusters were all similarly shaped. I moved in for a close look and saw that each had the telltale separation where two shells of a clam were joined together. That night we had the savory meat of a new kind of rock scallop to spice our meal of fish. However, these same reefs were covered with rock oysters, which could be detected by a green moss growing from their shells. We had missed these and learned about them only when a native fisherman asked if we had found any oysters. It taught me a valuable lesson. From that time on I have always taken advantage of the advice and knowledge of local fishermen and divers.

The California abalone is so well camouflaged that it looks like just another rock. You can spot the abalone in the picture below by the row of inch-long black feelers and the lacy fringe of its foot protruding beneath the shell. (*Photo by Mick Church*)

Some sea creatures practice camouflage by burying themselves in the sand. To the untrained eye of the sightseeing diver, a sandy ocean floor looks like an empty desert, barren of any life. To the trained eye of the hunter, it can be a bonanza of sea food, thriving with sea shells and fish. The hunter knows that delicious clams live permanently under the sand and are bivalves with a siphon tube extending to the water. He locates his quarry by looking for these tubes. Other telltale signs are "whiskers" or odd pieces of seaweed that appear to be growing from the sand but are actually attached to a buried shell. Many choice shells crawl out of the sand to feed at night and bury themselves during daylight. These usually leave a track in the sand which a trained hunter can recognize and follow to its source.

Fish, such as halibut, flounders, rays and sand sharks are often buried, or partially buried, and many a diver has been startled out of his face mask when one of these fish exploded in front of his eyes. They can be recognized by the shapes of their bodies beneath the covering of sand. Often only a projecting fin, the tail, or just the mouth and eyes may be showing. A trained eye recognizes these signs and can usually tell the identity of the animal before it is disturbed. But sometimes even the experts are deceived and, occasionally, a case of mistaken identity can produce some unexpected thrills and excitement.

One such incident which I will always remember occurred while I was hunting fish off Refugio Beach, California, 30 miles north of Santa Barbara. It was on the Fourth of July, the state park was crowded with vacationers and our activities had attracted a large audience of curious spectators. It turned out to be one of those rare days when the water was crystal clear, but the reefs were empty of sea life. This is a strange phenomena for which I have yet to find a satisfactory answer. One day a reef will be swarming with every type of animal, the next day, nothing. Why they leave and where they go is a mystery for which there are a multitude of theories including everything from tides, currents and temperature changes to a full moon and a lack of food supply. But none of these satisfactorily explain why rock-dwelling creatures, who establish a more or less permanent home in the caves and crevices of a particular reef, would all simultaneously disappear. But, it happens often. And this day we were faced with the prospect of disappointing our admiring audience by returning to shore with empty fish stringers. That's when I spotted the sand shark, or rather, what I mistakenly believed was a shovel-nosed sand shark.

There are a number of sharks which lie in the sand and sleep during the day. Two on the West Coast which are found partially buried are the shovelnose (or guitarfish) and the angel shark. The guitarfish has a long, thin body, wedge-shaped head, and a small mouth placed far back under its pointed nose. This shark is harmless and skin divers find sport in grabbing them by the tail and wrestling them to shore. The angel shark is another story. Its body is shaped like a bass fiddle, complete with a slender tail that causes it to be occasionally mistaken for a ray. The mouth of the angel shark is a horizontal slash across the front of its head and, when it opens its mouth, it looks as if the whole head has opened up to gulp in its prey. Skin divers who know what they are doing can grab small angel sharks by the tail and, by dexterous handling, can manage to keep from being bitten. But they grow to a huge size and the really big ones are nothing to fool with.

We were free diving without air tanks and the crowd was still watching us, so I decided to give the spectators a thrill by grabbing the sand shark and hauling it to shore. I swooped down behind it, grabbed the tail and gave a mighty tug. The whole bottom of the ocean seemed to explode from the sand. There was a tug of tremendous power. Then I was hanging onto the tail of the largest angel shark I have ever seen. Its great body was longer than mine and almost as wide as it was long. I had about as much control as if I had had a Brahma bull by the tail. The shark did a "U" turn and the front half of its body headed toward me. The open mouth was so big that it looked as if I could swim into and out of it without touching the sides. With a yank on its tail, I pulled myself up along its body away from that monstrous open mouth. By the time the shark finished its turn, I was halfway to the surface and heading in the opposite direction. I guess this shark was sluggish with sleep. It decided to let me go and settled back to the bottom to finish its nap. After that I investigated carefully before attacking camouflaged sea animals.

Probably the disguise that deceives more skin divers than any other is the ability of some types of fish to change their coloring to blend with the surrounding background. Flounders are notorious for this.

Skin divers who know what they are doing can grab small angel sharks by the tail and, by dexterous handling, can manage to keep from being bitten. Mike Swanson prepares to try his luck while diving off Santa Cruz Island, California. (*Photo by Paul Tzimoulis*)

A spotted moray eel takes refuge among coral branches. Such now-you-see-it, now-you-don't tactics make a novice skin diver think he is stalking shadows. (*Photo by Paul Tzimoulis*)

One scientist said that, if you placed a flounder on a checkerboard, in no time, you could be playing checkers on its back. Others are equally effective. The giant grouper, or sea bass, of tropical waters is a prime target for spearfishermen. They grow to several hundred pounds and are usually found in caves and holes. But often they will be resting quietly on a sand or gravel bottom. At these times, their coloring blends so completely with the surroundings that even other fish are deceived into coming too close. The grouper's mouth is a tremendous cavern that fills with water when it is opened wide. Unwary fish swimming within range are caught in a torrent and are swept into the open mouth. To the casual diver a grouper in ambush looks like another bump in the sand and he is often surprised when, with a thump of its great tail, a giant fish takes off under his nose. A common experience of divers hunting among the coral heads of tropical waters is to hear a series of such tail-thumping reverberations as a school of grouper are flushed from their lairs. The sound carries a long distance through the water and serves as a warning signal, alerting fish throughout the area. Once this chain reaction starts, the chances of finding a sleeping grouper are very slim and other tactics must be employed.

Another fish that can change colors with lightning speed is the ling cod of North Pacific waters. They reach weights of well over fifty pounds and are a prime quarry for skin divers. A hunter stalking one of these fish underwater may actually see it change coloring as it passes from shadow to sunlight over different types of bottom. Other fish use color cells to create patterns on their skin which make them difficult to see. One fish in the Caribbean adopts vertical bars that blend with coral branches when it is motionless. But when it moves, the bars are changed to horizontal stripes that are equally confusing. Such now-you-see-it, now-you-don't tactics make a novice skin diver think he is stalking shadows.

The needlefish, pipefish and trumpeter fish of tropical waters, hide their long, slender bodies in clumps of gorgonia, sea fans and coral so they look like one of the branches. They blend so completely with their background that, even when you know where one is hanging, it is difficult to distinguish until it moves. Another type of needlefish is colored light blue and its body is almost transparent. They hover in the top-few inches beneath the surface of the water, where the sun's rays flickering on surface ripples make them practically invisible. I tried to photograph a school of these fish in the waters of Cozumel Island off Yucatán. Although my camera was within three feet of the fish when I snapped the shutter, nothing showed in the slides but sunshine and surface ripples. The only reason I could see them was that my eye picked up movement where the camera couldn't.

Some of the rockfish, such as the sculpin, stonefish and cabezon adopt both the shape and coloring of their surroundings. Lying in the rocks, sand or coral, the irregular shape of their bodies and the mottled coloring of their skin make them look like a bump on the bottom. A few of these can be a real danger to unwary divers. Their spines pack a poison that can cause excruciating pain if bumped or touched. The spines of the stonefish inhabiting coral reefs of tropical waters, carry the most poisonous venom of any known sea creature, and a diver accidentally putting his hand on one of these ugly animals must be treated as if bitten by a poisonous snake.

Camouflage is only one of the forms of defense and offense developed by marine animals. All creatures in the sea, from tiny plankton to the giant sharks and sperm whales, are surrounded by enemies and are subject to attack from the moment they are born. The law of "survival of the fittest" reigns supreme and the mortality rate of those which make a mistake or are unlucky is appalling. For example, a female spiny lobster, or crayfish, twelve inches long, will lay 500,000 eggs, and only a very few of these ever reach maturity. Other creatures are even more prolific. It has been estimated that, if every herring egg were to reach maturity, and each reproduced in the same abundance, the sea would be so full of herring you could walk across the water on their backs. The young fry are under attack not only from strangers, but often from brothers, sisters and parents. A sea animal that has survived in such a hostile environment has learned all the tricks of his trade and has become extremely alert to any sign of danger. When we consider that most of the specimens a skin diver is hunting have had ten to fifteen years experience and some are more than one hundred years old, it is easy to appreciate the need for skill and an understanding of the environment. When you enter the underwater

A scuba diver moving slowly and carefully through gorgonian coral is accepted by a school of reef fish. (*Photo by Paul Tzimoulis*)

Three hunters prowl Palancar Reef, at a depth of 60 feet, off Cozumel Island, Mexico. (*Photo by Ron Church*)

arena in search of game you must not only learn to swim like a fish, you must act like a fish and think like a fish. Experienced hunters call this developing a "fish sense." It means that you will not only learn the places your game are most likely to be found, you will learn the time of year and the time of day they frequent the area. You will know if they move in on a high or low tide, when they feed and what they eat and which are their natural enemies. You will be able to penetrate their camouflage, detect their hiding places and even anticipate their movements. With practice, your eyes will become so accustomed to detecting telltale signs of movement, shadows, shapes and coloring, that spotting them will be as automatic as detecting traffic signs and hazards while driving on a freeway. It is an area where curiosity pays big dividends. Every odd formation or strange shape that catches your eye or does not blend perfectly with the terrain should be carefully investigated. Every shadow or shape that moves against the current, or is out of time with the rhythm of the surge and sunlight, should be closely watched until you are satisfied of its identity. The curious diver will check every hole, cranny, crack and cave. And the rewards for his curiosity will be a full game bag, or at the least he will see things that the casual diver misses.

Author Barada "drops in" for a lobster hunt off Catalina Island, California. In addition to the usual assortment of equipment used in scuba diving, he wears a decompression meter on his left wrist to measure the rate of gas absorption by his body and so help him to avoid the bends. (*Photo by Paul Tzimoulis*)

2   *Rules of the Road*

IT IS natural that old-timers should feel a nostalgia for "the good old days" when skin diving was so new that just going underwater made us pioneer "frogmen" and we felt like heroes exploring a new world. But, when compared to the opportunities available to the modern skin diver, those days were far from good. The equipment that was available in "the good old days" was crude, poorly made and so unreliable that its failures often got us into trouble. But our greatest handicap was a colossal ignorance of even the most fundamental safety rules of diving, and the laws which governed our survival in this new environment. The rules for sport diving were not yet written, no precedents were established and there were no authorities or instructors to guide us and pave the way. We were forced to learn the hard way, by getting into trouble and working our way out of it, and too often we learned a major safety rule because the diver who violated it did not survive. This learning process was slow, and often very painful, and our ignorance of the environment tempered and restricted our understanding and enjoyment of its opportunities.

The "golden days" of diving are really just beginning and I envy today's novice who is young enough to take full advantage of the opportunities that underwater activities now have to offer. Divers today are aided by modern, sophisticated equipment which has evolved over the years and is backed by thousands of hours and thousands of dollars in research and engineering to insure reliability. Even more important, by utilizing the professional instruction courses available throughout the country, the many instruction books on skin diving, and the services and guidance of professional dive shops and diving organizations, a novice can learn more in a few months than I learned in twenty years. I am frequently amazed to discover that a seventeen- or eighteen-year-old diving student often knows as much about the physics and physiology of diving as I do, and can discuss intelligently the problems and precautions inherent in deep-water work. Give this youth a few more years and he will know and understand more about the world's oceans and their inhabitants than an old-timer ever could, and his enjoyment of diving will increase in proportion to his knowledge.

On the other hand, I am sometimes appalled to find a new skin diver who ignores the information and instruction available to him and insists on trying to learn the hard way, on his own. In my opinion this is just as foolish as a person trying to learn to swim by jumping off a boat in mid-ocean and heading for shore; or a person who starts learning to drive by jumping into a car and heading onto a Los Angeles freeway. The standard statement by people who insist on trying to dive without instruction is, "I'll be careful." This is blatantly foolish. Careful of what? They don't know the rules, what the dangers are, or the simple steps required to avoid trouble.

The undersea is a safe and friendly place, yet man is out of his element when underwater. He must learn a new set of nature's rules and laws which are not encountered on the surface. The greatest danger to skin divers is ignorance of these rules. Learn and practice them, and the underwater world will welcome you with unending fun and interest. Break them, and the result may be a painful and frightening experience. The old cliché that "ignorance is bliss" simply does not hold true for skin diving.

This book is not intended as an instruction manual. Other books, some of which are recommended in the bibliography, when used in conjunction with diving instruction, will give you the information and teach you the skills required to start diving. This chapter can present only a cursory introduction to the fundamentals which must be learned thoroughly before diving is attempted.

One of the things you should know before you rush out and buy a set of diving gear is that some people cannot dive at all. If you have any serious built-in handicaps, a physician should be consulted before you go underwater. Diving demands a considerable amount of physical exertion, plus the ability to make rapid adjustments to pressure changes. If you are so out of shape that climbing a short hill sets you to puffing and blowing, stay out of the water until your physical condition is improved. If you have heart, lung, ear, nose, sinus or bronchial trouble, subjecting your body to sudden changes in pressure may cause serious injury. Your doctor is the one to give you advice.

Probably the greatest contributing cause to diving accidents is overexertion, followed by panic. So, learn your limitations and stay well within them. Always pace yourself and retain a reserve of energy in case of emergency. Build confidence by practicing skills under the supervision of an instructor, so you can stay calm when trouble develops.

There are two major categories of diving. One is free diving (without breathing apparatus) in which you hold your breath while you are underwater. The other is scuba (self-contained underwater breathing apparatus) diving in which a supply of high-pressure air is carried in a cylinder on your back. With or without breathing equipment, diving is basically swimming underwater and, the better you can swim, the better you can dive. Watermanship, not swimming form, is most important. A diving instructor would far rather train a student who is "at home in the water" than a person with excellent swimming form who doesn't know how to relax and take it easy. A diver surfacing with an empty tank may be required to swim a long distance back to shore or a boat. In this case, the idea is just to stay afloat. Speed or hurry can cause overexertion.

Free diving while holding your breath can be attempted on your own, without instruction, but learning will be slow and you can expect a few knocks. However, if you are a strong swimmer and handle yourself well in the water, there is very little danger of getting into serious trouble. This kind of diving is similar to swimming and diving without equipment of any kind, except that the mask, flippers and snorkel make swimming on the surface and underwater almost effortless. A free diver does not have to worry about bends, embolism, narcosis or other diving illnesses which are encountered only when breathing air under pressure. However, some of the equipment you must become familiar with and learn to use properly can be mastered much more quickly under the guidance of a certified instructor, or an experienced diving buddy. And one of the basic safety rules is "Never Dive Alone." However, two beginners diving together is similar to the blind leading the blind.

The basic equipment you must master as a free diver is:

Face Mask: Allows you to see underwater as clearly as you see in the air.

Swim Fins: Give an amateur the swimming ability of an expert and leave your hands free for handling equipment.

Snorkel: Permits you to breathe *on the surface* without lifting your face out of the water. Lets you rest and relax without treading water.

Surface Float: A platform towed or pushed by the diver, used to carry extra gear and as a rest station.

Inflatable Float (or emergency float): (Not to be confused with a surface float.) Worn by the diver and equipped with a cartridge for emergency inflation, or a mouthpiece for inflation under normal circumstances.

Diver's Flag: To signal boats that a diver is working in the area. Required by law in many states.

Diver's Knife: Worn at all times while in the water. Not intended for defense but used as a cutting, digging or prying tool. A safety item in case of entanglement.

Gloves: Should always be worn by salt-water divers to protect hands from sharp or stinging marine organisms.

Exposure Suits: Wet suits made from closed-cell sponge rubber; keep you warm when swimming in cold water. Should be worn when diving in water temperatures below 70 degrees.

Weight Belts: Lead weights worn to counteract the buoyancy of wet-suit material. When properly weighted, a diver has neutral buoyancy underwater. Weight belts must have quick-release buckles that can be operated with one hand.

Spear guns: (Covered in detail in Chapter 5)

Cameras: (Covered in Chaper 2)

Do not use ear plugs: Dangerous to use and never worn by skin divers. They prevent pressure equalization and can cause ruptured eardrums.

Becoming familiar with each of these pieces of basic equipment, and practicing the techniques of free diving while holding your breath will make scuba diving much easier and more fun to learn. You will be amazed at the feats you can perform and, when you do start using scuba and breathing underwater, you will be less apt to panic if something goes wrong. An experienced free diver who suddenly loses his air supply while diving with scuba is in a familiar situation and is less apt to make a mistake than a scuba diver who has never been underwater without air. Also, the confidence gained from free diving will allow you to concentrate on learning scuba and the laws of changing pressure rather than worrying about a lot of strange equipment.

A novice is far less apt to get into serious trouble while he is holding his breath than he is with scuba. Your inherent caution and the natural warnings built into your body will prevent you from go-

Free diving while holding your breath can be attempted without instruction, but learning will be slow, and you can expect a few knocks. (*Photo by Paul Tzimoulis*)

ing too deep or staying too long, and ascending rapidly will cause you no problems.

This is not true with scuba. Its operation is completely automatic, and, once you become accustomed to it, breathing underwater is so natural that you will unconsciously probe much deeper and stray into areas that would be impossible to reach by free diving. There is no sensation of depth, and very little sensation of time or direction. You are as free as a bird with the ability to roam in three dimensions and your equipment will take you as far and as deep as you wish—as long as your air supply holds out, or something doesn't go wrong. Most mistakes by inexperienced scuba divers are made either while ascending or on the surface, often after they have used up their air supply. These mistakes are almost invariably caused by ignorance of basic diving rules or fear and panic caused by lack of proper training.

The basic equipment for scuba diving is a cylinder, or cylinders, of high-pressure air, approximately 2000 to 2500 p.s.i. The standard tank holds 71.2 cubic feet of air (NOT OXYGEN OR ANY OTHER GAS MIXTURE) and weighs approximately 35 pounds out of water, but is practically weightless when submerged. It is the weight of an empty cylinder which causes trouble for divers on the surface. In normal swimming with your head out of the water, the cylinder is partially above the surface and its weight tends to drag you under. Use a snorkel so you can swim with the cylinder submerged or an inflatable vest to hold your head out of the water.

The heart of scuba operation is a demand regulator which automatically reduces the high-pressure air from the cylinder to breathing pressure. A mouthpiece is attached to the regulator, either directly in a single hose, or through flexible breathing tubes in double-hose models. A back pack or harness straps the cylinder to your back. All you need to do is attach the regulator to the tank valve, turn on the air and start breathing. The regulator adjusts automatically to the changes in water pressure as you dive, so you always inhale air that is compressed to exactly the same pressure as the water. As you go deeper, the air you breathe is more compressed and is used up more quickly. A standard cylinder will last approximately 1½ hours on the surface (depending upon how hard you are working), 45 minutes at a depth of 33 feet, 30 minutes at 60 feet, and 22½ minutes at 99 feet and so on down. The reasons for this are explained under gas laws. Because depth and time are extremely critical to the duration of your air supply and diving safety, wearing a depth gauge and a diver's watch is recommended, and a novice should use a cylinder equipped with a reserve valve which gives him a few minutes warning before he is completely out of air. A pressure-proof gauge attached to your regulator which tells you exactly how much air is left in your tank at all times is an excellent accessory.

There are two kinds of laws governing our behavior, nature's laws and those that are made by man. Unlike man-made laws which can be broken with impunity as long as you don't get caught, you can't break one of nature's laws and get away with it. The laws governing the behavior of compressed gases which affect diving safety are natural laws, and if they are ignored, no matter who you are or what your excuse, the results are positive, often painful and sometimes fatal. There are no policemen, lawyers, judge or jury to which you can appeal, and often there is no second chance. When dealing with these laws, ignorance is absolutely not excused so you had better know what you are doing *before* you dive with scuba.

It is not our intention to give detailed information on the gas laws in this chapter, and reading this material certainly does not prepare you to try scuba on your own. Our purpose is only to point out the need for more complete information, and enable you to appreciate more fully some of the incidents described in this book.

A diver is not only concerned with the pressure exerted by the weight of water he is under, he is also concerned with the weight of air in the atmosphere surrounding the earth. At sea level the weight of air is 14.7 p.s.i. This is expressed as one atmosphere of pressure. Each 33 feet of sea water also exerts a pressure of 14.7 p.s.i., or one atmosphere of pressure, so we can measure the effect of compressed gases on a diver in terms of atmospheres of pressure, keeping in mind that we are talking always about absolute pressure which includes the weight of the atmosphere. Boyle's law tells us that the volume of a gas at constant temperature varies inversely as the absolute pressure. This means that if the pressure on a gas is doubled, its volume is reduced one half. A depth of 33 feet is equal to two atmospheres of absolute pressure so, a balloon inflated on the surface

Becoming familiar with each of the pieces of basic equipment, as worn by this diver, will make scuba diving much easier to learn. (*Photo by Paul Tzimoulis*)

would be compressed to one half its volume if taken 33 feet underwater. Conversely, a balloon fully inflated at a depth of 33 feet and sealed, would expand to twice its volume if floated to the surface, and probably would burst.

The same thing will happen inside a scuba diver's lungs if he holds his breath on the way to the surface. The expanding air can rupture lung tissue, and, if escaping bubbles enter his blood stream, he suffers from aero embolism, which in some cases is fatal. This is the reason for the number one rule of scuba diving: *Never Hold Your Breath During Ascent.* You should continue breathing normally, but if your tank is completely out of air, *Exhale As You Ascend.*

Boyle's law also tells us how long the air in a scuba cylinder should last. It requires twice as much air to fill your lungs at 33 feet as on the surface, so your tank will only last half as long. At 66 feet (3 atmospheres), your tank will last one third as long and at 4

With scuba you are as free as a bird, with the ability to roam in three dimensions, and your equipment will take you as far and as deep as you wish—as long as your air supply holds out. (*Photo by Denis Brand*)

atmospheres (99 feet), it will last one fourth as long or about 22½ minutes. Of course a relaxed diver who is taking it easy will get almost twice as much time from a tank as a nervous or frightened diver, or one who is working hard, so cylinder times can only be based upon the average person's air consumption under normal conditions. That's why you need a pressure gauge to eliminate the guesswork.

The action of pressure upon other air spaces inside our body is also governed by Boyle's law. Fortunately, most of our body is liquid which is unaffected by pressure changes. It is the other small percentage that occasionally gives us trouble. These are ears, sinus, lungs and sometimes cavities in teeth. These spaces must be pressurized as you descend, and any slight difference in pressure will be noticed immediately. If you feel any pain in your ears or sinus, stop your descent, rise to a more shallow depth and stay there until they are cleared by holding your nose and blowing, or by swallowing. If you cannot clear your ears and sinus, you can't dive.

The squeeze of water pressure also affects the buoyancy of wet suits which compress as you go deeper. So, less weight is worn on deep dives than when working shallow. It affects inflatable floats because a cartridge that will blow up a vest on the surface may not have enough volume at 100 feet or deeper. Conversely, a float inflated on the bottom may rupture during ascent and leave you on the surface with no float.

Other gas laws have physiological effects on a diver's body which can cause serious injuries if ignored. Fortunately these problems are only encountered when working in comparatively deep water and are usually of no concern at depths above fifty feet. But you will be amazed at how easy it is to get into deep water, so every scuba diver must know these laws and how to use them.

One of these laws is that pure oxygen is poisonous to humans when breathed under pressures greater than two atmospheres. Because air becomes more dense when it is compressed, the partial pressure of oxygen in air increases and ordinary air becomes toxic at great depths. But, of more immediate importance to scuba divers, is the absorption of gas into their tissues while they are underwater.

Henry's law states that the amount of gas which will dissolve in a liquid at a given temperature is almost directly proportional to the partial pressure of that gas. This means that if the pressure is doubled, a liquid will absorb twice as much gas. If the pressure is tripled, a liquid will absorb three times as much gas, and so on into the depths. This law explains the causes of "the bends," nitrogen narcosis, CO_2 poisoning and other diver's illnesses.

Although nitrogen is a neutral gas, its slow absorption by body tissue when subjected to pressure is of definite concern to divers. If you are deep enough for a long enough period of time, the nitrogen absorbed into your body must be released very slowly or it will foam out in a froth of bubbles which cause the painful "bends." The depths and times permitted for diving without stopping for decompression while the gas escapes from your system are listed in the United States Navy Decompression Tables, available in almost every book on diving. These tables also list the depths and times required for decompression stops when maximum bottom time is exceeded. When calculating bottom times, you must count the total time underwater, from the time you leave the surface until the time you leave the bottom, and your depth is the deepest point reached on any dive. Total time is the combination of all dives within a 24-hour period. The rate of ascent from any scuba dive, with or without decompression, is at 60 feet per minute. Exceeding this can cause lightheadedness, et cetera. At slower rates your body continues to absorb nitrogen.

Nitrogen narcosis is simply a technical name for diver's drunkenness caused by the narcotic effects of nitrogen absorbed by your body. It affects divers differently, some are more quickly narcotized than others, and the reactions of each diver are different. Also, the same diver may be hit with narcosis one day and not be bothered the next. A common misconception of narcosis is that it hits suddenly at a particular depth. This is as logical as saying that one particular swallow of liquor makes a person suddenly drunk. Diver's drunkenness comes on gradually, a little at a time, as you descend. Its effects are usually not noticeable above depths of 100 feet, and, for most divers, are not of much concern above 150 feet. However, like being a little bit drunk, a slight case of narcosis is like a few drinks before driving. There's no harm done unless you get into trouble, or into a situation that requires a cool head and fast reactions. A bad hit with narcosis

One of the advantages of scuba is that it gives you the ability to explore deep submarine caverns which exist along almost every shoreline in the world. (*Photo by Mick Church*)

is serious only because a drunken diver is a menace to himself and everyone associated with him.

CO_2 poisoning is an illness that scuba divers usually need not worry about. It is the result of an abnormal build-up of CO_2 in the blood stream, which is of great concern to helmet divers who breathe within an enclosed air space. However, CO_2 build-up can occur in scuba diving from overexertion while breathing from a regulator which delivers an inadequate air supply. If you plan on deep diving, with heavy exertion on the bottom, buy a regulator that will deliver a minimum of 22 cubic feet per minute air flow with only a slight suction effort.

As stated in the beginning of this chapter, I strongly recommend that a novice diver take full advantage of the diving organizations available to help him become acquainted with the underwater world. Some of the most active of these are:

DIVING INSTRUCTOR ORGANIZATIONS
Contact these groups for a certified instructor in your area.

NATIONAL ASSOCIATION OF UNDERWATER INSTRUCTORS (NAUI)

NAUI PACIFIC
P. O. Box 7506
Riverside, California 92503

NAUI ATLANTIC
P. O. Box 12277
Ft. Lauderdale,˙ Florida 33314

NAUI CANADA
P. O. Box 264
Willowdale, Ontario, Canada

THE YMCA SCUBA COMMISSIONERS
1. MAINE YMCA—173 Main St., Waterville, Maine 04902
2. NEW HAMPSHIRE YMCA—P. O. Box 476, Concord, New Hampshire 03302
3. NEW ENGLAND AREA YMCA—14 Somerset St., Boston, Mass. 02108
4. NEW YORK STATE YMCA—2 West 45th St., New York, N.Y. 10036
5. PENNSYLVANIA YMCA—907 North Front St., Harrisburg, Pa. 17105
6. CENTRAL ATLANTIC AREA YMCA—P. O. Box 508, Princeton, N.J. 08540
7. INTERSTATE YMCAS of the CAROLINAS—400-A East Morehead St., Charlotte, N.C. 28202
8. SOUTHERN AREA YMCA—1611 Candler Bldg., Atlanta, Ga. 30303
9. OHIO–W. VIRGINIA AREA YMCA—40 West Long St., Columbus, Ohio 43215

10. MICHIGAN YMCA—301 West Lenawee St., Lansing, Michigan 48914
11. INDIANA YMCA—310 North Illinois St., Indianapolis, Indiana 46204
12. ILLINOIS AREA YMCA—19 South LaSalle St., Chicago, Ill. 60603
13. NORTH CENTRAL AREA YMCA—Suite 220, 915 W. Wisconsin Avenue, Milwaukee, Wisconsin 53233
14. WEST CENTRAL AREA YMCA—3301 Van Buren St., Topeka, Kansas 66611
15. SOUTHWEST AREA YMCA—3012 Maple Avenue, Dallas, Texas 75201
16. PACIFIC SOUTHWEST AREA YMCA—715 S. Hope St., Los Angeles, Calif. 90017
17. PACIFIC NORTHWEST AREA YMCA—909 Fourth Ave., Seattle, Wash. 98104

LOS ANGELES COUNTY DEPARTMENT OF PARKS AND RECREATION
Underwater Section
155 W. Washington Boulevard
Room 1202
Los Angeles, California 90015

PROFESSIONAL ASSOCIATION OF DIVING INSTRUCTIONS (PADI)
P. O. Box 13
Morton Grove
Illinois 60053

SOUTHWEST COUNCIL OF INSTRUCTORS PROGRAM (SCIP)
Hilton Quine
2714 Wesleyan Street
Irving, Texas 75060

UNDERWATER SOCIETY OF AMERICA
Bourse Building
Room 492
Philadelphia, Pennsylvania 19160
(*for a diving club or council in your area, most of which provide instruction or can tell you where to get it*)

DIVE SHOPS
Listed in the yellow pages of telephone books

The skilled underwater hunter stands out from a group of average skin divers like a professional baseball player among a bunch of amateurs. (*Photo by Jack McKenney*, Skin Diver *magazine*)

3 *Relax and Enjoy It*

THE SKILLED underwater hunter stands out from a group of average skin divers like a professional baseball player among a bunch of amateurs. Even when swimming on the surface he is as fluid as the medium he is in and his actions are almost as effortless as a fish. He has learned that water is 800 times thicker than air and moving through such a dense atmosphere requires a different set of rules from on the surface. Once these rules are learned, the underwater world is a relaxing, restful place where gravity can be ignored and a diver can soar in three dimensions as weightless as a feather. Adjusting to the languid tempo and drifting with its rhythm brings a release from tension and a rapport with sea creatures that less-skilled divers find difficult to understand. But, the diver who brings the hustle and bustle of surface life into the submarine environment and attempts to do things in a hurry, is penalized by exhaustion and constant frustration in his search for game.

Old Cap Watkins of the Santa Monica Life Guards was a classic example of a man in perfect rapport with the sea. When I was first learning, Cap was seventy years old and already had forty years experience at skin diving and lifeguarding. He was as much at home in the water as a seal. Watching him perform was like watching an underwater ballet; Cap could always teach the younger divers a few new tricks any time he went out. An example of his prowess occurred with a group of gung-ho divers off Santa Cruz Island, California. As soon as the boat's anchor touched bottom the eager beavers hit the water and flippered off as if racing for a New York subway. Cap waited until the commotion died down, then leisurely strapped on his gear, slipped over the side, and drifted to the bottom right under the boat. A half hour or so later the other divers were back on board with empty scuba cylinders, and the entire group had only a few fish and one or two lobsters to show for their efforts. It was another half hour before Cap bobbed to the surface and he had more lobsters, fish and abalone than all of the eager beavers put together. His air had not only lasted almost twice as long as the other divers, but he had found an abundance of game where they had reported it to be sparse and elusive. His secret was slow motion and a control of body movement that permitted him to glide through the water and position himself with no unnecessary waving of arms, legs, feet and hands.

Fish are extremely sensitive to movement, especially quick motions that are out of tune with the surroundings. Your actions should be slow and deliberate. Any hesitation or nervous wiggling will be communicated to the fish as a signal of possible danger. That this can happen even with a skilled diver was illustrated by an experience in the big-fish tank at Marineland of the Pacific.

The fish in this tank are conditioned to aquarium life and are so tame that a diver can swim close enough to pet them with his bare hands. The grouper on the bottom are usually so sluggish that you practically have to push them out of the way before they move. My assignment was to get a picture of a girl and a grouper staring at each other, with the grouper's head a few inches away from the girl's mask. My model was an excellent diver who had many hours underwater as an instructor for the Los Angeles County Department of Parks and Recreation. We talked over the assignment on the surface,

A good test of your "fish sense" is to take some choice morsels of food underwater and see if the larger fish will eat out of your hand. (*Photo by Chuck Nicklin*)

and in the water I demonstrated what I wanted her to do by putting my face so close to the grouper that the glass of my mask practically bumped its nose. But it was a day of constant frustration. We spent almost three hours underwater and burned up two tanks of air without getting the picture. The girl never managed to get closer than two or three feet before the frightened fish moved out of the way. Her apprehension was displayed by small, nervous motions and irregular breathing which was communicated to the fish as a sign of danger.

The fact that some divers seem to radiate a warning of approaching danger while others seem to be accepted as a part of the environment is one of the facets of acquiring a "fish sense" that is not clearly understood. A good test of fish reaction to your diving techniques is to take some choice morsels of food underwater and see if the larger, more wary fish will move close enough to eat out of your hand. If even the small fry refuse to take your bait, you have a serious problem and should examine your entire attitude toward skin diving. Only the most apprehensive and nervous diver with little control over his body movements will have trouble feeding tiny fish. If the small fry take your offering and the larger fish continue to stay out of range, the chances are that your breathing is erratic or some portion of your body is moving too much. Some divers believe that fish are wise enough to recognize a spear gun as a source of danger and stay out of range when they see a diver carrying one. However, I suspect that most divers, when stalking fish with a spear gun, literally radiate warning signals which frighten wary fish. I believe that fish have a sixth sense that detects a diver's tension or apprehension regardless of warning movements or noise.

There are no magic formulas or high-speed expressways to learning the watermanship and techniques of a skilled underwater hunter. Like any other sport, skin diving requires practice to develop the necessary skills and accumulate the knowledge. Everything else being equal, the man who spends the most time in and under the water will become the most proficient. This writer is convinced that the fastest and most efficient way to develop proficiency as a hunter is to leave the breathing apparatus on shore, and learn to stalk game underwater while holding your breath.

There are two basic methods of diving and hunting. One is skin diving, or free diving, where you hold your breath while you are beneath the surface. The other is with scuba, an abbreviation of self-contained underwater breathing apparatus, where an air supply on your back permits you to descend to greater depths and stay submerged for long periods of time. Both have advantages and disadvantages. Scuba is best in deep water and in some conditions where hunting by free diving is out of the question. Skin diving is best over a shallow bottom where heavy surf or surface turbulence makes scuba diving extremely hazardous. Also skin diving is far more effective in a comparatively shallow area where a wide expanse of bottom must be covered. The free diver's hunting time in the water is not limited by the amount of air in his tank, and he is free to roam over a tremendous area of reef in search of game. It is not uncommon for a team of skin divers to kick out from the beach and spend five or six hours in the water exploring miles of reefs before returning to shore.

The hunter without breathing equipment is free to roam for hours and cover miles of reef before returning to shore. (*Photo by Paul Tzimoulis*)

Some types of game fish are so wary that a scuba diver's exhalations and bubble noises alert them to danger and keep them well out of range. These fish are practically never taken by scuba diving and can only be approached by a skin diver who has learned to hunt underwater with the stealth and craftiness of a seal. But, probably the greatest advantage of developing proficiency by skin diving is that, to be effective while holding your breath, you must learn to employ many tricks and techniques that a scuba diver seldom learns. Most of these can be utilized when using scuba and will make hunting with breathing equipment more enjoyable and more effective. Not the least of these is breath control and economy of body movement, both of which are prime requirements for any kind of diving.

Most people believe that holding your breath long enough to dive to the bottom and hunt game underwater is a feat reserved only for top-notch athletes. This is a common misconception which a little practice over a shallow reef will correct. If you can swim and can hold your breath for 30 seconds, you can stay underwater long enough to stalk and spear a fish or capture lobsters and sea shells. The first thing you must learn is to relax completely while you are on the surface. Use your snorkel for breathing, let the water support your weight, and rest, moving with the least possible exertion. If your arms, legs or flippers are in constant motion, or if your head is always bobbing above the surface, the length of time you can hold your breath will be drastically reduced. Practice moving through the water without letting your flippers break the surface. Keep them submerged. Your kick will be more efficient and you will avoid alerting timid game. This is especially true when stalking fish over a shallow bottom. The splashing of flippers on the surface creates a noise that can be heard long distances underwater and any skittish fish in the area will be frightened away. Your surface dive is also very important. Watch a group of skin divers and you can tell the old-timers by the way they submerge. A novice tends to waste a lot of energy getting started for the bottom which uses up valuable underwater time. He also does so much splashing and kicking that the turbulence frightens away all but the most curious fish. Take a tip from seals and sea lions, and learn to submerge with hardly a ripple. You can do this only if you take it easy. And hurrying downward will only use up energy and shorten the time you can stay on the bottom. An example of this occurred during a trip to Cozumel Island off Yucatán in the Mexican Caribbean.

We had emptied our scuba tanks early and were finishing the day skin diving for crabs and lobsters. One of the members, a powerful swimmer with a build like Charles Atlas, joined me and we worked the reef together. The bottom was 30 to 40 feet deep, but the water was crystal clear and we snorkeled on the surface looking for ledges and cracks in which our quarry could be hiding. My companion was in constant motion. With arms and legs waving, he flippered around me like an anxious dog on the end of a leash. When I found a ledge and dived, he zoomed past me to the bottom, took a quick look, and returned to the surface before I reached the coral. Several times he spotted a crab or lobster, missed with a fast grab, and surfaced leaving the quarry still sitting in the crevice. After I had several lobsters and a couple of crabs tucked safely into our goody bag he commented, "Boy, you sure hold your breath a long time. I watched you from the surface and had to take two or three breaths before you came back up." On board the boat this diver could hold his

The intricacy and beauty of the living coral can be appreciated from this close-up photo of brain coral. (*Photo by Paul Tzimoulis*)

The experienced diver moves in slow motion, with as little effort as possible, to conserve his air and give him time to hunt. (*Photo by Paul Tzimoulis*)

breath for two minutes, but underwater his time was limited to a few seconds. The reason, of course, was his constant motion on the surface and his terrific expenditure of energy when he dived. He had learned diving with scuba and had never had to relax and conserve his air supply which is so necessary when free diving.

An experienced skin diver seldom expends much energy on the surface. He uses this time to rest and relax, breathing deeply with forced inhalations and exhalations to clear his blood stream of carbon dioxide and charge his lungs with a fresh supply of oxygen. Your rate of breathing depends upon the amount of energy or exertion you are expending. Oxygen is the fuel your body burns to generate energy, and carbon dioxide is the waste product of this combustion. The urge to breathe comes from a nerve center at the base of your brain which is triggered by the amount of carbon dioxide in your blood stream. When you work hard, more oxygen is consumed and more carbon dioxide is generated. Circulation and breathing speed up to supply the extra demand. Trying to hold your breath after this speed-up has already started is asking the impossible. In the water, even a slight amount of exertion has an exaggerated effect upon your ability to hold your breath. This is especially true if you ever hope to attain a respectable depth.

The inexperienced diver will automatically make the mistake of increasing the speed of his descent according to the depth he hopes to attain. The deeper he intends to dive, the faster he descends. The experienced diver knows better and his reaction is exactly the opposite. He may power to the bottom in shallow water where he can hold to the reef and relax after he gets there. But on a deep dive he moves in slow motion, coasting downward with as little effort as possible so he will have air and time left to hunt before returning to the surface. The more you practice free diving the deeper you can go and the longer you can stay underwater. Constant deep breathing expands the capacity of your lungs and practice at holding your breath trains your brain to ignore early carbon-dioxide warnings. This is why many skin divers can stalk and spear fish at fanastic depths of more than 100 feet.

However, when diving deep, slow motion on the way to the surface is even more important than on the way down. If you run out of air on the way to the bottom, you can always turn around and go back for more. But, if you hurry on the way up, oxygen consumption speeds up and you may lose consciousness before you reach the surface. This is called "shallow-water blackout," a real threat when diving to great depths while holding your breath. It is what spearfishing champions mean when they talk about the ordeal of the "long, slow climb" back to the surface. A skin diver, hurting for air on the bottom, must savagely fight a natural instinct to race madly back to the top. I learned this lesson while hunting white sea bass off Catalina Island, California.

The white sea bass is one of the game fish most highly prized by Southern California divers. Its silvery, white body reaches lengths of over six feet, with weights of more than eighty pounds, and it is one of the most wary and most difficult to approach of all the fish in the sea. I was skin diving on the outer edge of the kelp beds, when a great beauty almost four feet long slipped out in front of me and headed toward the bottom. I followed, slowly at first, being careful not to startle or frighten the fish by moving too fast. The sea bass was unhurried, drifting lazily downward, but always just out of range of my spear gun. It was a tantalizing experience. With each stroke of my flippers, I hoped to get close enough to pull the trigger, but, as I gained speed so did the fish, constantly maintaining that foot or so of distance that would make my harpoon fall short of its mark. My full attention was concentrated on the target and I lost all sense of depth and time. Caught in the hypnotic trance of "white-sea-bass fever," I was being teased into going deeper than I had ever been before. The fish finally gave a flip of its tail and darted away and I became painfully aware of my predicament. I was only a foot or two off the bottom, my lungs were already screaming for air, and the surface looked as far away as the moon and the stars. My first reaction was to make a mad dash upward. But years of experience gained control and I started a steady kick of my flippers for the "long, slow climb" back to sunlight and air. The swim seemed to take ages. My throat and lungs burned and every muscle in my body quivered and ached for lack of air. As I neared the surface, bright-colored lights began flashing in front of my eyes. I became dizzy and a great weariness swept over my body. The last ten or fifteen feet were negotiated in a daze of semiconsciousness, with only instinct helping me to maintain a kick with my flippers. Nothing, before or since, has ever tasted as sweet as the air I gulped after that dive. I am confident that, had I hurried the ascent, I would never have reached the surface.

The slow motion and conservation of energy, which is so important while snorkeling on the surface, becomes even more important when you are on the bottom. Racing through the water at high speed may be fine for TV heroes while chasing underwater villains, but it is worse than useless when hunting fish. Even the slowest fish is so much faster than a skin diver that trying to catch one makes about as much sense as a bulldozer racing a sports car. Also, their reactions are about four times faster than yours, so, if you hope to surprise them, you must use your head as well as your hands.

Stalking fish underwater is very similar to stalking deer in a forest. You will see a lot more game while sitting quietly on the bottom or hanging motionless above a reef than you ever will while swimming aimlessly from rock to rock. Like all wild animals, fish are instantly alerted by unusual movement or strange noises. Often they will swim close enough to investigate the source of the disturbance. But, if it appears threatening or dangerous, they stay out of range or slip quietly away before the diver ever sees them. From a fish's point of view a diver charging toward it with hands and flippers threshing, bubbles streaming, and the great eye of a face mask staring at it is probably the most frightening apparition it has ever seen. You will see evidence of this every time you go hunting with a companion who has not yet learned the quiet approach.

A friend of mine complained of seldom seeing a decent fish, and when he did, could never get close enough to spear one. I agreed to help, and since he was comparatively new at diving and unskilled as a free diver, we strapped on our tanks and went into the water off Catalina. It was an average day with visibility of 25 to 30 feet. I drifted to the bottom in about 50 feet of water, caught hold of a rock to steady myself, and waited quietly for my friend to join me. The usual assortment of calico bass, sheepshead, kelp bass and perch circled my position, peeking at me from behind clumps of kelp and playing hide-and-seek around the rocks, all well out of range of a spear gun. In the distance I caught glimpses of the shapes of larger fish circling in the fog-fringe of dimness at the limit of our field of vision. After a few minutes, I looked up to see my companion still hovering 15 feet above the bottom. I motioned him to join me. When he hesitated, I swam up and pulled him down to the rocks. It took a little time for him to realize that the idea was to let the fish find us instead of us hunting them. But he finally got the message and settled down to wait, impatiently, for something to happen. The fish gradually lost their apprehension and began moving in to look us over. Once my friend leveled his gun at a perch, but I stopped him before he pulled the trigger. I had seen a large sheepshead weaving through the kelp just out of range of a spear gun. If we waited a little longer, this fish's curiosity would overcome its caution and we would get a shot. But I forgot about my companion's inexperience and pointed to the fish before it was in range. He saw the fish and took off after it as hard as he could go. The fish veered away and my friend followed in hot pursuit. He burned up his entire tank of air as

that wise old sheepshead led him a merry chase around every rock
and kelp bed on the reef. Later, on board the boat, I explained that
I had been watching the fish all the time and, had he waited a minute
or two longer, it would have moved close enough for an easy shot.

It is possible to approach within range of a jittery fish, but not by
chasing it pell-mell across the bottom. Move as slowly and cautiously as a cat stalking a gopher, and take advantage of any cover
that is available. If the fish is playing cat-and-mouse around coral
heads, rocks, or kelp, move more quickly while you are hidden from
its view. Most fish cannot see directly behind them and, when one is
swimming straight away, you can sometimes come close within range.
But be ready to shoot the instant the fish turns, or it will be gone
before you can blink your eyes.

The experienced hunter investigates every grotto, crack and crevice in search
of hidden game. (*Photo by Paul Tzimoulis*)

A skin diver can also take advantage of a fish's conditioning to its normal dangers. The predators, such as larger fish, seals and sharks, feed only when they are hungry, and some only at certain times of the day. It is not unusual to see sharks, barracuda, seals and large game fish swimming peacefully amidst schools of small fish which seem unconcerned by their presence. I have watched fish swim in perfect safety a few inches in front of the nose of sharks which made no attempt to attack. This is why a skin diver who emulates the predators by pretending to be on a peaceful mission, can get close enough to spear a nervous fish. But, let the fish sense that it is in danger, and you will be lucky to see it before it disappears.

If a skin diver waits for clear water before he goes hunting, he will spend most of his time on shore. Except for a very few places, such as the Florida Keys and the offshore islands of Southern California, the waters of the Continental United States have very poor visibility. Contrary to popular belief, even some of the most popular diving grounds, such as the Pacific and Atlantic coasts, are far from clear, and it is a rare day when a diver can see farther than 20 feet. This is even more true of inland lakes and rivers where if you can see 10 to 15 feet, diving is considered excellent. Divers in these areas either learn to hunt by "blind diving," when they often can see less than six feet, or they spend all of their underwater time in the Caribbean or the Gulf of California where the water is almost always clear.

Dirty water is not such a handicap as it may seem. You may not be able to see the breath-taking beauty and seascapes of tropical coral reefs, but you often have better hunting than clear-water divers. There are a number of reasons for this. Turbid water is often caused by a plankton bloom which fills the water with tiny, microscopic organisms. Plankton is the basic food of the sea upon which forage fish such as anchovies, sardines and herring depend for food. When the bait fish thrive, their abundance attracts schools of larger fish which are sought by skin divers. The waters around Hawaii and in the South Pacific, although crystal clear, are noted for their sparsity of game fish. They are also almost devoid of plankton. The waters along the Pacific and Atlantic coasts are rich in plankton, and are some of the most productive fishing grounds in the world. To a cer-

Joyce Irwin brings in a large grouper speared while free diving off Isla Mujeres, Yucatán. (*Photo by Mick Church*)

tain extent the same thing holds true in fresh-water lakes in which spearing rough fish such as carp and suckers is permitted. These fish thrive on algae which clouds the water, and the dirtier the water, the better the hunting. Of course, if dirty water is caused by pollution, the number of fish is drastically reduced because most pollution is poisonous to sea life. This is why diving and fishing is usually poor in harbors and near big cities.

At first glance the suggestion that pollution is converting the world's oceans into a giant cesspool seems absurd. But the signs are already appearing to those who care to look. When we consider that giant bodies of water, such as Lake Michigan and Lake Erie, are already the world's largest cesspools, and that the population explosion has only just begun, the prospect of a polluted ocean is not too far fetched. The damage is not caused so much by sewage as by industrial chemicals. For example, minute amounts of some chemicals in sea water will kill fish and marine creatures. Our cities are dumping billions of tons of these chemicals into the sea every hour of every day, and with most of them the poisonous effects accumulate and last indefinitely because they are never absorbed or broken down. I started diving the Southern California coast over thirty years ago and have watched it gradually disintegrate from a submarine garden, lush with vegetation and teeming with sea life, into an underwater wasteland. Many of the reefs which were once covered with seaweed and thriving with abalone, lobsters and scallops are now barren, and a ring of empty, dead shells on the bottom bear mute testimony to the fate of its inhabitants. A tiny, flickering ray of hope lies in the government's increasing interest in the oceans and its belated concern over pollution. But, if politicians and history repeat past performances, we can't expect meaningful action until a major catastrophe occurs.

Also, dirty-water diving can be more productive than clear water because every fish you see is within range of your spear gun. This doesn't mean that slow motion and careful stalking are not important. A fish can detect your presence long before you can see it and turbulence or fast movements will keep them out of sight. The best way to hunt in turbid water is by prowling the bottom and checking every hole, crevice and cave for hidden fish. In fact, this is a good way to hunt in any kind of water. The technique is simple. Just drift quietly to the bottom and pull yourself along by holding to the rocks or coral. You can cover a lot of bottom with a minimum of exertion, and you are in constant control of body movement, and you need not even use your flippers. When you come to an interesting ledge or hole, maintain body control by holding to the rocks and pull your head into its shadow. While your eyes remain in the sunlight you will be able to see only a few inches into a cave. But with your head inside the entrance, your eyes adjust to the shadows and sometimes an innocent-looking hole will turn into an underwater apartment house inhabited by all kinds of sea creatures. Some of the world champions hunt holes and caves so thoroughly that they carry an underwater light to search out fish hiding far back in the shadows.

Another method which is effective in murky water is to sit quietly on the bottom and wait for a fish to come within range. It is equally good for both skin and scuba diving and can often produce fish in the dirtiest of water. When water is so dirty you can see only three or four feet, your range can be increased by lying on the bottom and looking at the surface. Fish swimming overhead will be silhouetted against the sky, often offering a perfect target.

Van Laman, Australian woman's spearfishing champion, surfaces with a 78-pound brown, spotted cod she speared while free diving in the Swain Reefs. Van won the championship when she was 18 years old. (*Photo by Ben Cropp*)

Occasionally, no matter how carefully you follow the rules for stalking fish, or how expertly you employ the tricks and techniques for coaxing a prime fish into range of your spear gun, your best efforts will be frustrated by a visit from an unwelcome guest. An example of this occurred while I was stalking a grouper in the waters off Bimini in the Bahamas. It wasn't a huge fish, only about 30 pounds, but it was the largest one I had seen all day and I was working patiently to entice it within range. The water was about 30 feet deep over a sandy bottom which was spotted with small coral heads. I was skin diving, and the fish played hide-and-seek with me for about half an hour. It moved slowly but cautiously around the coral heads, curious, but always staying just out of range. I played dead, sinking to the bottom and lying motionless as long as I could hold my breath, watching the fish out of the corner of my eye. Next, I pretended to dig choice treasures out of the sand. Then I tried breaking off small pieces of coral and inspecting them as if it were my only interest. These tactics held my fish's curiosity but failed to bring it in. Finally, in desperation, I laid my spear gun on the bottom and pretended to inspect a piece of coral with both hands. That did it. The grouper started to move closer. I remained still until it disappeared behind a clump of coral only ten feet away. Then I picked up the spear gun, ready to fire the instant its head appeared. Suddenly, the sound of a surging splash jarred the tranquillity. I looked up to see a boat overhead and an unknown diver emerging from a mass of bubbles his noisy entry had created. His was the classic boat entry, jumping over the side with his feet spread wide. The technique put him into the water safely with all his gear intact. But the noise frightened every fish in the area and I never saw the grouper again. This diver had been watching me from shore and had come out to see what I was doing. After a few minutes I decided to call it a day. With the kind of disturbance he was creating, our chance of even seeing a spear-size fish was mighty slim.

This illustrates why skilled spearfishermen are so reluctant to buddy dive with a person they don't know. It may also explain why a spearfisherman often acts unfriendly when you approach him in the water. You may have been the unwelcome guest that frightened away a choice fish he had been stalking for an hour.

Stalking fish with a camera requires the same skills, techniques and "fish sense" as when hunting with a spear gun. Dewey Bergman demonstrates the art of getting close. (*Photo by Paul Tzimoulis*)

4   *Shoot, But Not to Kill*

STALKING fish with a camera requires the same skills, techniques and "fish sense" as when hunting with a spear gun, and for many divers it is more rewarding and challenging than shooting to kill. The game you shoot with a camera is not destroyed and the pictures preserve its grace, beauty and color forever. No license is required for hunting with a camera, and all fish in all waters are legal for the photographer. In addition to the same fishing license required for rod and reel, most states have spearfishing regulations which specify which waters are legal for underwater hunting, and the species of fish you can legally take. With a camera, as with a spear gun, the trick is to get close before you shoot, and the closer the better. Water acts as a filter, absorbing both natural light and artificial light almost like a sponge absorbs water. The range of visibility of cameras and film is even less than that of your eyes and a "long shot" underwater is seldom more than ten or fifteen feet even under ideal conditions. Add to this the plankton and particles normally suspended in the water

Snapping the shutter at the exact instant the action takes place is more difficult underwater because everything including the cameraman is moving, and it is impossible to yell directions. (*Photo by Bill Barada*)

and the effect is very similar to taking pictures in a heavy fog. Contrast and resolution are often lost because subjects are so fogged-in by the water that background and details "gray out." This is especially true when using black and white under natural light, but it also holds true for color. And the only answer is to stalk your quarry until you are close enough for details to register, usually six feet or less, depending upon the clarity of the water and the brilliance of surface sunlight.

A skin diver taking snapshots with a still camera must catch his subject at the exact instant the action takes place. This means that he must have his camera correctly focused, the aperture adjusted and the action framed to give a pleasing composition, then snap the shutter just when everything has come together in the proper perspective. Accomplishing this in a fluid medium while you, the water, the fish and your diving buddy are all moving in three dimensions is a little like trying to take pictures while riding through a forest on a bicycle. It utilizes all of the skills of an experienced diver, the knowledge and techniques of a skilled underwater hunter and an ability with a camera that can be acquired only by practice. We don't mean to imply that underwater photography can only be enjoyed by expert photographers who are also experienced divers. The average shutterbug can have a ball taking snapshots while skin diving, just as he can on the surface, and the simple "aim-and-shoot" cameras so popular for topside pictures are available for the same kind of operation beneath the surface. But, even with a foolproof camera you can waste a lot of film and time unless you learn a little about underwater photography before you start snapping the shutter.

It is not the purpose of this chapter to teach you how to take pictures while skin diving or to give detailed information about the various kinds of cameras and equipment available. For this we refer you to any of the excellent books on photography listed in the bibliography, and to *Skin Diver* magazine for companies specializing in this field. However, since hunting sea creatures with a camera is very similar to other types of hunting, some understanding of the principles involved will be appreciated.

Almost any make or model of camera available for surface photography, both still and motion picture, can be used underwater if sealed in a pressure-proof housing. Accessories for these cameras, such as flash, strobes, photo floodlights, light meters, etc., can also be used when diving if they are properly protected. But, unlike surface photography where a wealth of complicated accessories and gadgets can be utilized effectively, the key to a good underwater camera is simplicity of operation and handling. Remember that your visibility is restricted, even in extremely clear water, and all numbers on dials, gauges, meters, etc., must be large enough and clear enough to read through your face mask in dim light. Also, you will be floating upside down almost as often as you are upright. Swimming amidst kelp, coral or seaweed, with a string of accessories dangling from your body like ornaments on a Christmas tree, will be inviting entanglement.

The simple aim-and-shoot cameras so popular for topside pictures are also available for underwater. Housings for the Instamatic, such as the one shown above, are priced from $25 to $30 and can be purchased at any dive shop. (*Photo courtesy Ikelite Co.*)

Most skin divers prefer cameras and gadgets that have negative buoyancy so they hang downward in the water rather than float out of sight above their head. Also, a buoyant piece of equipment will "fall" to the surface if it is dropped and cannot be laid on the bottom while you are busy with something else. A small object floating to the surface is usually never found because it drifts away in the current, or is hidden by waves and chop. Whenever possible, your accessories should be attached firmly to the camera housing and equipped with control knobs and levers large enough to be manipulated with cold fingers encased in heavy gloves.

A high-quality camera will give better results underwater just as it does on the surface, providing it is encased in a housing as good as

Almost any make or model of camera can be used underwater if sealed in a pressure-proof housing which should be custom made to fit the individual camera. The price depends upon the material used and the type of camera. Most dive shops can order custom housings. (*Photo courtesy Mako Products, Inc.*)

the camera. Many divers have made the mistake of trying to cut expenses by encasing their cameras in cheap housings and, if they didn't leak, the controls gave them so much trouble they were lucky to get a picture. Amateurs, when building an underwater housing, often overlook the fact that it must be pressureproof as well as waterproof. The mistake is so common that even large manufacturers have fallen victim to it. An example of this occurred a few years back when a company marketed a universal camera housing in the form of a bag made of tough, flexible plastic. The instructions were to put your camera inside the bag, seal the opening to prevent leakage, and manipulate the controls from the outside by feeling through the flexible plastic. This worked fine in swimming pools, but when taken to depths

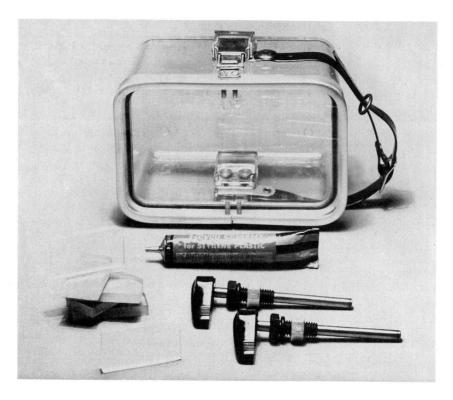

Do-it-yourself kits are available for building your own camera housing. Prices range from $18 to $25, and are available through skin-diving shops. (*Photo courtesy Ikelite Co.*)

greater than ten feet, water pressure squeezed the plastic around the camera so tightly that none of the controls could be manipulated and the camera was useless.

Many camera cases that work fine in bathtubs, swimming pools and extremely shallow water fail when taken into deeper water because the effect of pressure has not been anticipated. Square Plexiglas cases with large surface areas have a tendency to bend under pressure, which may cause them to leak at the corners. Extensions of camera controls, which project through the housing to permit operation underwater, have been known to jam when subjected to pressure and become very difficult or impossible to operate.

These are a few of the reasons why a good camera housing often costs more than the camera itself. The engineering know-how re-

The larger film sizes such as the Rolleimarin give sharper and more detailed pictures underwater just as they do on land, but they are bulkier and usually more expensive. This camera and housing will retail between $800 and $1000. Sold through camera stores and dive shops. (*Photo courtesy Honeywell Inc.*)

quired to produce a dependable and efficient housing is learned only from experience. The best housings are usually designed by a diver-photographer who is familiar with the problems. You can build your own camera housing. Do-it-yourself kits are available, with most of the critical engineering already done for you. But, unless you are willing to do a lot of research and like to work with complicated gadgets, I suggest you select one of the many excellent cameras or housings that have proved themselves through the test of actual usage. Good underwater pictures are difficult to obtain under the best of circumstances. Handicapping yourself with poor equipment can bring early discouragement.

Excellent housings are available in either Plexiglas or cast aluminum for most motion-picture cameras, both 8 and 16mm. and for

2¼ ×2¼ and 35mm. still cameras. The advantages and disadvantages of the two sizes are the same in submarine photography as on the surface except they are probably more exaggerated. The larger film sizes will give sharper, clearer pictures with greater detail, which is a definite advantage when shooting underwater. But these cameras are larger, heavier and more expensive both to purchase and to use. A major consideration when selecting a motion-picture camera is whether you hope to use the footage for television or motion-picture release. If so, you have no choice but to film in 16mm. at sound speeds of 24 frames per second. This is the smallest film that is acceptable for commercial broadcasts even though the new super 8mm. films project ex-

I believe that motion pictures are easier to shoot underwater than stills. But only a professional such as Stan Waterman can produce films that everyone enjoys. (*Photo by Bill Barada*)

cellently in large auditoriums. The cost of shooting 16mm. color film is approximately four times greater than 8mm. so, unless you have definite plans to show your film on television, you can have a lot more fun on the same amount of money with an 8mm. camera.

I believe that motion pictures are easier to shoot underwater than stills. There are fewer adjustments to contend with and you can follow a continous action until it reaches "the decisive moment." With a still camera you must snap the action at the exact instant or it is gone forever. However, the type of photography you choose is a matter of personal preference and the use for which it is intended. Motion pictures can be a lot of fun to shoot and, if well done, they may entertain your friends and relatives for a few showings, and may even find a free slot on TV. But good still photographs, both color and black and white, have a thousand uses and their value lasts indefinitely.

When selecting a still camera, the higher cost of 2¼ ×2¼ film as compared to 35mm. is a factor, but probably the major objection is that fewer pictures can be taken without reloading. Changing film is a simple matter when you are walking around on shore. But when you run out of film while diving, it means returning to the surface, swimming back to your boat or to shore, drying the housing, and removing the camera before you can get at the film. Going through this a few times while you are dressed out in diving gear is the best incentive I can think of for using a smaller camera, or carrying extra cameras and taking a tender to change film for you.

Another argument in favor of 35mm. cameras is that one model, designed by Captain Jacques Cousteau, does not require a housing. It is the essence of simplicity, no larger than an ordinary 35mm. camera, but it can be used both on the surface and underwater to depths of 180 feet. This camera was originally marketed under the trade name "Calypso," but is now manufactured and distributed by Nikon under the name "Nikonos." Most top-notch underwater photographers prefer a high-quality, single-lens reflex camera to the Nikonos. But, for the average diver, its simplicity and ease of handling make it very attractive, and it can produce some excellent results once you have learned how to use it.

As we said earlier, water absorbs light almost as effectively as a sponge absorbs water, and sharp pictures can be obtained only by

The Nikonos II, developed from designs by Jacques-Yves Cousteau, is the essence of simplicity, requires no housing and can be used both on the surface and underwater. Camera with accessories sells for a little over $200. Available through skin-diving shops and camera stores. (*Photo courtesy U. S. Divers Co.*)

getting as close to your subject as possible. Another phenomena affecting photography is that objects seen in the water through a face mask are magnified in size, so everything you see appears to be one third closer and one fourth larger than it actually is. Water has the same effect on a camera lens as it has on your eyes, so the size of an object six feet away will appear in the photograph as if it were shot from a distance of only four feet. With a normal lens, this magnification reduces the field of vision similar to that of a telephoto lens in the air. For this reason, practically all underwater cameras are equipped with a wide-angle lens, and most photographers agree that the wider the angle, the better. This is because an extremely wide-angle lens will give you a wide field of vision at extremely close range.

The magnification of objects underwater also affects your judgment of distance. The camera "sees" objects as if they were one third closer, and the camera controls must be set for this distance. This problem does not bother experienced skin divers who have learned to judge distance correctly. But it can be very confusing to a novice whose pictures are consistently out of focus or overexposed.

Probably the single, most frustrating problem in trying to take pictures underwater is the constant fight to obtain contrast. A dark-colored fish photographed against a background of coral, rock or seaweed, blends so completely with its surroundings that it is almost invisible. Even brightly colored fish and other sea creatures have a tendency to blend with the background, and a skin diver dressed in a black rubber suit is almost completely lost among kelp or dark-colored rocks. This is not such a problem in shallow water, above ten or fifteen feet, because the full spectrum of sunlight penetrates to register on your film. Of course the depth that light will penetrate, both horizontally and vertically, depends upon the clarity of the water, the time of day and your geographical location. Cloudy water absorbs light much more rapidly than crystal clear water and sunlight will penetrate deeper when it is almost vertical than when it strikes the water at an angle. This is why in clear, tropical waters under an almost vertical sun, it is possible to take natural-light photographs at depths as great as 200 feet. However, a universal problem that causes loss of contrast at any depth, is the filtering effect of water upon the warmer colors of the spectrum. Reds, yellows and oranges are absorbed very quickly and, although these colors are present on the bottom, all that you or your camera will see are the blues and greens. To test this, dress a buddy diver in a red vest and follow him as he descends. The red will gradually turn to orange, then yellow and finally into a bluish-green that blends with the water and surrounding background. The depths at which these changes occur depend upon a number of varied factors, but if you go deep enough in any waters, these warm colors completely disappear and even your buddy's face and the blood from a wound appear blue-green. With only these colors available, your black-and-white pictures will be lacking in contrast, and your color pictures will all have a blue-green cast. You can increase the contrast by positioning your subject against a contrasting background. But you can't do anything about the color unless you take an artificial-light source down with you.

Underwater lighting for motion-picture cameras is expensive, cumbersome to use and is not readily available. Unless you are filming professionally or have a lot of money and time to spend on your hobby, lighting for motion pictures is not very practical. Artificial light for

Al Giddings and Dewey Bergman use flash to bring out the color which otherwise would not show, even in the crystal clear waters of Tahiti. (*Photo by Bill
Barada*)

A skin-diving shell collector reaches for a Triton Trumpet at the 100-foot hole off Waikiki, Hawaii. (*Photo by Ron Church*)

5   *Shellfish and Sea Shells*

THE SKIN diver with a taste for sea food or an interest in collecting sea shells will find a bonanza waiting for him on the bottom of the sea. Sandy beaches and rocky reefs of all the oceans are teeming with mollusks which are easy to find once you know what to look for and where it is most likely hidden. Non-diving shell hunters must comb the beaches after a storm, or stumble over rocks and coral in waist-deep water, hoping to find an exotic sea shell tossed up by the waves or washed into shallow water. And clam diggers must wait for low tide to invade the beaches and grope blindly in the sand and rocks for succulent shellfish. The skin diver can pick his days almost at random because his hunting ground is the relatively calm, deep water beyond the surf line. Here, in their natural habitat, the choicest specimens of sea shells can be found, undamaged by sun, sand and surf and usually in perfect condition. Many of the species considered rare by shore collectors are found in abundance by skin-diving shell collectors. Many of the exotic sea foods which command a high price in restaurants and fish markets are everyday table fare for skin divers who live near the sea coast. Even the more common clams, scallops and oysters take on a new and exciting taste when caught with your own hands. Modern food processing, quick freezing, instant packaging and jet airplanes have made fresh sea food available in all parts of the world. But nothing can match the flavor of shellfish brought fresh from the sea and popped directly into the cook pot.

Diving for sea shells is the easiest type of underwater hunting. Except for the outer shell which houses the animal, their only defenses are camouflage and hiding and, if any of their natural enemies had the hands, fingers and brain of a skin diver, there would be few sea shells left in the oceans. They can't escape once their hiding place is discovered. Most species are found in shallow water, less than 50 feet deep, and they can be hunted when the water is turbulent and murky. But until you learn to penetrate their camouflage and learn their hiding places, you can spend hours scouring the bottom and see little but sand, rocks and coral.

The best way to learn how and where to find sea shells, or anything else in the ocean, is to go with someone who knows. If you don't have a friend who is proficient at shell hunting, the local dive shop is your best source of information. It can usually put you in touch with a local skin-diving club and most have members who are avid shell collectors. But much of the knowledge must be gained from shell books and from experience. It would take a book much larger than this just to list all of the different species of sea shells, and this chapter can only give a few guidelines on how and where to find some of the most popular kinds. More complete information can be obtained from shell books listed in the bibliography.

Large, heavy shells such as conch, tritons and helmets, which lie on the surface of the sand and depend upon their thick shells as protection, are easy to find and identify. Their only attempt at deception is a few barnacles and organisms clinging to the shell which could lead you to think they are a rock or piece of coral. Others, such as the giant abalones and delicious rock scallops of the Pacific coast, are a different story. Their deception is so effective that experts often overlook them and, even when one is located, there is no assurance that you will bring it to the surface. Trying to show a diver, unfamiliar

Diving for sea shells is the easiest type of underwater hunting. (*Photo by Paul Tzimoulis*)

The giant kelp off Southern California clings to rocks on the bottom at depths as great as 100 feet, and the strands drift upward to float their leaves on the surface. (*Photo by Chuck Nicklin*)

with west coast surf and kelp beds, how to find abalone can lead to some interesting experiences. A description of diving conditions in the abalone beds will give you an appreciation of the problem.

The giant abalone is found only along the Pacific coast of California and Mexico and connoisseurs consider it one of the most delicious of all shellfish. There are several species with mature shells, ranging in size from five inches in diameter for the smaller "blacks," to as much as fourteen inches for the larger "reds." Only one half of the body is shell. The other half is a tough muscle, or snail-like foot, which clings to the rocks of a reef with a powerful suction. The meat is solid muscle which, when sliced into steaks, pounded until it is tender, then dipped in an egg batter and fried, is a gourmet's delight. Abalone steaks bring a high price in restaurants and meat markets throughout California. But the supply is limited, and laws prohibit its sale outside the state. Even so, the abalone fishery supports a multimillion-dollar industry, larger even than the lobster fishery, and commercial divers can make big money when they hit a productive bed. Abalone are favorite targets for skin divers and their delicious flavor is responsible for attracting thousands of new converts to the sport. Beginners are successful at hunting for these shellfish in the calm, clear waters of offshore islands. But a skin diver who can produce abalone consistently along the mainland coast can find shellfish in any waters in the world. A combination of heavy surf, tremendous swells, thick kelp beds and murky water create conditions so unfamiliar to the uninitiated that visiting skin divers often have trouble just learning to handle themselves in the water. Some are kept so busy trying to keep from being tossed around over the bottom by the surge that they haven't time to bother looking for anything. Others become seasick while snorkeling on the surface and watching the bottom rise and fall as it sweeps back and forth beneath their eyes. But those who have become adept at free diving, know not to fight the surge and quickly learn to let themselves drift back and forth with the rhythm of the swells. Until a diver becomes expert at handling himself in heavy surf and surge he will be wise to restrict his diving to calm days and protected areas where turbulence is at a minimum. But some wave action and turbulence are common to all ocean diving. It is the huge kelps beds and jungle of seaweed that give visiting divers the most trouble.

The giant kelp is as unique to California as the abalone itself. Its spores, or hold-fasts, cling to rocks on the bottom at depths as great as 100 feet and the strands sweep upward through the water to float their leaves on the surface. These forests may be small, individual patches, or tremendous beds extending for miles over the surface of the ocean. They are the spawning grounds and hiding places for fish, and the reefs beneath them are the best places to look for lobsters and abalone. To a skin diver looking at this tangled mass for the first time, swimming into it appears to be the height of folly. Often, especially at low tide, the leaves of a healthy kelp bed form a dense, impenetrable mat on the surface. Beneath it the growth is thin, similar to the trunks of trees in a forest, with open spaces through which you can swim. The trick is to keep your body, and all equipment, underneath the surface mat. Skin divers, when coming up for air in the kelp, part the surface strands and allow only their snorkel to protrude. Everything else stays underneath. The only way a spectator can spot an expert in a kelp bed is by the spout of water that spurts into the air as he clears his snorkel. His body never shows except when he is putting a catch into a game bag attached to his surface float. Occasionally, when swimming in heavy kelp, a strand or two will get hung up on your equipment. This is nothing to worry about. Live strands are watery and brittle in texture and can easily be broken with a snap of your fingers. The kelp beds offer some of the most interesting diving in the world and the only real danger is fear and panic, which causes a person to thrash around in desperation, so he becomes hopelessly tangled.

Learning to dive in kelp is only the first step toward becoming a proficient abalone hunter. As we said before, recognizing one when you see it and learning to get it off the rocks can pose problems for the novice. Don't expect to see the gaudy-colored, polished shell so common in souvenir shops. The living shell is covered with the same marine organisms as the rocks to which it clings, and is as difficult to see as a pearl on a sandy beach. Telltale signs are a combination of its shape, a circle of short feelers or suction tubes surrounding a feeding shell, a small space between the shell and the rock, or a row of holes in the shell that serve as suction-relief ports. At times all of these signs can be seen at once, but usually only one or two will be visible

Sea shells are easy to find if you know where to look. This diver has discovered a prize sea snail clinging to a leaf of giant kelp. (*Photo by Denis Brand*)

Rock scallops are larger and more delicious than bay scallops, yet are never found in restaurants. Dick Barada displays a giant taken in Baja California, Mexico. (*Photo by Bill Barada*)

and then only if your eyes are close enough to the rock to recognize details. And don't expect to find shells out in the open. These have been picked by other divers long ago and, unless you are working in virgin waters off Mexico or far-out islands, the only ones that are left are those that other divers have overlooked. These will be well hidden amidst the thickest tangles of seaweed or deep in narrow crannies which are easily missed. So, finding abalone is a question of bottom prowling and investigating every nook and slit. When you do find one, use the correct technique or you may well wind up by leaving the shell still clinging securely to its rock.

It is the powerful suction of the abalone that often defeats an untrained skin diver. When first sighted, the shell will be lifted slightly off the rock allowing the siphon tubes to extend and feed. At this point an abalone iron or any prying tool, such as a heavy diver's knife, screwdriver, etc., can be slipped under the edge of the shell to pry it off. If this is done quickly, the abalone will pop off before it has a chance to clamp down. But, at the slightest disturbance, the shell clamps tight to the rock and you will have a struggle to get it free even if you succeed in getting a prying tool under the shell.

While skin diving off Laguna Beach, I met a tough Marine whose stubborness matched that of an abalone. He was an excellent swimmer and skin diver with experience in the South Pacific, but he had never seen an abalone. I pointed out a few, showed him how to pry them off the rocks, then swam the short distance to shore and watched him from the beach. I could tell he had found something when he started making continuous dives in the same spot. He struggled with it for over half an hour, his head bobbing to the surface only long enough to get his breath, then disappearing as he continued his silent battle with an object on the bottom. Finally the diving ended, and the Marine headed for shore. He was in shallow water near the beach before I noticed that he was struggling desperately and gasping for air. I grabbed my gear and dashed for the water, arriving just in time to see him rise up with a boulder in his arms that was twice the size of a basketball. He tossed the boulder at my feet with a disgusted expression and said, "There's your cotton pickin' abalone!" Sure enough, a small black shell was clinging to the rock with a grip of death. Fresh scratches and pockmarks on the rock, and chips off the edge of the shell, gave silent testimony of his underwater battle with this stubborn shellfish.

Abalone are certainly not the only *Mollusca* that can be hunted under the kelp beds and among the rocky reefs of the Pacific coast. The California molluscan province, bounded by the state of Washington to the north, and Magdalena Bay in Baja California to the south, has over 2000 species of shells. A similar situation exists along other shores. On the east coast, the Carolinian province between Cape Cod and the middle of Texas has almost 3000 species; and the Caribbean province has 1200, with more being discovered every day. Some of these shells are hunted as sea food, others for the splendor of the shell as a collector's item, and some for both the meat and the shell. The primary value of abalone is the delicious flavor of its meat, but nobody can ignore the gorgeous coloring and striking beauty of the shells, and an exceptionally beautiful specimen has started many an abalone diver into shell collecting. The same is true of clams, scallops, conch and others which are hunted primarily as food.

The conch is a staple food in the diet of natives in almost all of the islands of the Caribbean. Tourists visiting these vacation spots find the variety of conch on the menus of restaurants as common as beef is in America. You can eat conch steaks, roasts, stew, chowder, conch burger, and even raw in salads and cocktails, but no matter which form it takes, if properly prepared it is both delicious and nourishing. There are hundreds of varieties of these shells and diving for them is as easy as picking loose rocks off the bottom. They are large, snail-like shells that crawl slowly over sand bottoms, feeding on algae from grass beds. They cannot live in water colder than 70 degrees, and they like the shallow, protected areas inside a reef, cove or bay. When hunting them, look for grass beds growing on a sandy bottom in shallow water from 15 to 30 feet deep. The conch (*strombus*) will be triangular in shape, the helmet (*cassis*) round or oval. Both will resemble large barnacle-covered rocks or stones, so investigate every rock that is the right size or shape.

Many other shells which are hunted primarily for their meat are also treasured by shell collectors, and often it is difficult to decide which has the greater value. A meat hunter is not concerned with the problems of preserving the shell in perfect condition and often destroys it in order to get at the animal. One of these is the rock scallop which is found on the reefs and breakwaters of the Pacific coast. The rock scallop is hunted by bottom prowling in much the same manner as for abalone. It clings to rocks in the same fashion as mussels and barnacles, and is so difficult to remove that divers often break open the shell and take the animal, leaving half of the shell still firmly cemented to the rock. Knives, crowbars and even claw hammers are used to pry them free. Individual rock scallops sometimes weigh over five pounds and the meat is far superior to the mud scallops which are common in restaurants. To my knowledge, rock scallops are not har-

Pin-shell clams such as the one shown here are fun to hunt, delicious to eat and beautiful when cleaned and polished. This one was taken off Cozumel Island, Mexico. (*Photo by Mick Church*)

vested commercially, and are one of the delicious sea foods enjoyed almost exclusively by skin divers.

Most bivalves, such as scallops and clams, are found buried in mud or sand and are harvested commercially by raking or dredging the bottom of bays and estuaries. But clam digging also attracts sportsmen and is so popular that at extremely low tides, the beaches of clam-producing areas swarm with clammers. Dressed in hip boots and armed with rakes, shovels and clam buckets, this army can be seen on the coldest and foggiest mornings, probing the exposed sand for these delicious shellfish. This type of hunting is restricted to areas where

Many of the sea shells lying in the sand look just like another rock, and are easily overlooked. (*Photo by Paul Tzimoulis*)

great stretches of beach are exposed when the tide is low and the water recedes. Skin divers have no such restrictions. Their clam diving is unaffected by low tides or the steepness of the beach, and tremendous new clam beds have been discovered in deep water. These are never reached by anyone wading from shore. An example is the famous pismo clam, which for years was thought to exist only along the shallow, sandy beaches of Pismo Beach, California. Now, skin divers are harvesting pismos at Zuma Beach, Newport Beach, and in Mexico where none were known to exist before.

Bivalves, which bury in sand and mud, feed through a siphon tube which draws water and microscopic organisms into the shell. Diving for them, either as a shell collector or a meat hunter, is simply a matter of learning to spot these siphon tubes on the surface of the sand. All you will see is a small hole in the sand, or sometimes an odd formation that looks like a flower petal lying on the bottom. The clam is buried a few inches beneath this tube and can be dug out with almost anything, such as a knife, sharp stick, or even your bare hands. In a contest to see who could bring the first limit of clams to shore, the winning diver used no digging tool at all. He carried ten small, sharp sticks each about the size of a pencil. When he spotted a siphon tube he pushed the stick into the hole, the shell clamped to the end of the stick and he swam to the next clam. When all ten sticks were placed, he collected his clams by grabbing the protruding "handles" and swimming to shore with the clams still firmly attached.

Skin-diving shell collectors become as adept at reading shell trails in the sand as an Indian is at tracking game in the desert. Some of the most-sought-after species of sea shells live burrowed beneath the surface of sand or mud flats, coming out only to feed at night. Most of these shells leave a telltale trail which a sharp-eyed diver can detect and follow to its source. However, other marine animals such as crabs, fish, worms, etc., also leave sand trails and you can waste a lot of time unless you learn to tell the difference between a shell trail and that of other creatures.

Tom and Mary Davis of Scuba Point, Possum Kingdom Lake, Texas, tell of such an incident during one of their vacation trips to the Caribbean. They are experienced skin-diving shell collectors who spend each vacation in the Caribbean. This time they were accompanied by a new convert to the sport whose enthusiasm more than made up for his lack of experience. He was doing fine, tracking shells with scuba and placing captured specimens in a mesh bag carried with him underwater. Then one day he came up from a dive so excited he could hardly talk. He was on the trail of the world's largest shell. Its track was several inches deep and over a foot wide. He had tracked it until he ran out of air, but hadn't come to the end of the trail. His excitement was contagious. A shell that large might even be a museum piece. Tom went under and scoured the bottom but could see no monster-shell track. After half an hour of fruitless searching he finally decided that his friend had been following a deep furrow made by his own bag of shells as he dragged it over the sand.

Only experience can teach you to recognize the trails left by different types of shells, but a few general guidelines may save you a lot of wasted time. A sharply zigzagged trail is probably made by a crab. A double trail is likely caused by the pectoral fins of a fish, and a trail ending in a mound with a hole in the top will be a sea worm. Most of the terebras, or spike shells, leave a straight furrow two to ten feet long. Round shells leave wider furrows and often wander in circles. When you follow the right trail, a shell will be found buried at its end.

Shells are enjoyed and used for a thousand different purposes in every country in the world. They are used as a medium of exchange in place of money by some natives; fashioned into beautiful jewelry and striking decorations; sold as ornaments, souvenirs and playthings; studied by scientists and collected as a hobby. Until about fifteen years ago, shells were used almost exclusively in the manufacture of buttons. Now plastics have replaced shells in the button industry and only a few of the most beautiful have great value for ornamental decoration. The most outstanding of these is the mother-of-pearl shell of the South Pacific. This shell is not only the source of the most valuable and most beautiful pearls in the world, the shell itself is in such demand that the government of French Polynesia has initiated laws and seasons to preserve the species. Scuba, and other types of artificial-breathing equipment is prohibited and the pearl shells are still harvested by skin diving in the same manner they have been for centuries. The native Polynesians are as much at home in the water as they are on land and are probably the world's finest water people. A

Tahitian spearfishing team won the World Spearfishing Championships in competition with National Champions from countries all over
the world. A master mother-of-pearl diver in the Philippines told me
that native pearl divers can work at depths up to 200 feet and can
hold their breath as long as five minutes. While visiting the island of
Mooréa in French Polynesia, I watched ex-pearl diver Fariua Tehiua
drift to the bottom 120 feet below, stay there for almost a full minute
poking into holes and ledges looking for fish, and then surface without even breathing hard. Today the opening of the pearling season is
treated as a lengthy national holiday. Brawny, handsome young divers, shapely vahines (also spelled wahines), and entire families migrate to the designated island. The men dive for pearls all day, then
feast at a *tamaaraa* and dance the *tamure* at night until they become
so exhausted that they fall asleep. Then, refreshed, they start the
routine all over again. While the men are diving for pearl shells, the
women hunt sea shells, gorgeous cowries and delicate fan shells,
which they fashion into necklaces of "Neptune's Jewelry" later sold
to tourists or given away as a token of their affection.

For the full satisfaction of a rewarding hobby that will add new
meaning to your diving and put you in touch with fellow collectors
all over the world, you should follow the rules for shell collecting that
will make your specimens worthwhile. These rules are easy to set
down. Following them requires time, patience, and enough interest
to acquire the knowledge that gives any hobby its fascination.

The first rule is to learn the scientific names of shells. Not by mem-
orizing all at once, but one at a time, as they are collected. Common names are useless because the same shell may be called by different names in various parts of the world. Help in identifying specimens
can be obtained from books, shell clubs, museums, aquariums, col-
leges, etc.

The second rule is to keep accurate data. Shells without data are
just pretty playthings and worthless to a collector. Each shell in a collection must have the following information: date found, location,
type of bottom, depth of water, live-collected or a dead shell, and the
collector's name. If you know the correct scientific name, fine; but if
not, a trained collector can come up with the name from good locality
data. If you collect from one area all day, use one location grouping.

Shirley Church finds a tiger cowrie (*Cyprea tigris*) off Makua, Hawaii. (*Photo by Ron Church*)

But if you move to a different location, keep those shells separated.

The third rule is to learn where to find the kind of shells you wish to hunt, and what shells exist in your location, or the area you intend to visit. Books, shell clubs, etc., can give you a good idea of the shells available in a given area. Another good way is to walk the beach and watch for dead shells washed up from the bottom. These most always come from that location and live specimens will probably be found close by. Then learn the habits of different types of shells. If you know whether they are carnivorous, feeding on fish and other shells, or herbivorous, feeding on algae and plant life, you will have a better idea where to look for them. Learn if they bury themselves in the sand and can be traced by following sand trails. If they are nocturnal feeders, you will know to look for them at night with an underwater light. The rock dwellers, such as murex and chitons, will be hunted under rock piles on the bottom. Carefully turn over each loose rock and examine the bottom. Remember that over 70 per cent of the world's shells are less than one inch long, some as tiny as $\frac{1}{25}$th of an inch when fully matured, so a cursory inspection will miss choice specimens. Always replace the rock in the same position as you found it. If you leave the marine colony uncovered, it will be destroyed or eaten by small fish and the shell colony will be lost.

Ann Frame, an expert shell collector and skin diver, who conducts guided shell-collecting tours out of Marathon, Florida, gives the following advice to shell hunters visiting the Florida Keys. Ann says, "There are several do's and don'ts when going out shelling. Take several containers with you and keep shells from different areas separated, even though they are of the same species. A goody bag is fine for snorkeling, but you will need several plastic pails to transfer the shells into so you can keep them alive. Also take along a plastic, wide-mouth bottle filled with alcohol for preserving small specimens. Tough, plastic bags come in handy for separating fragile or special shells. Gloves are a must and I always wear a long-sleeved shirt and thin slacks or coveralls. The clothing not only prevents sunburn it also serves as protection from stinging coral and microscopic marine organisms."

The fourth, and most important rule of shell collecting is to properly clean and preserve shell specimens so you don't destroy their value or their beauty. Ann Frame's advice on shell cleaning is also worth repeating. Ann says, "There are many ways to clean shells. First remove as much surface dirt and growth as possible with a brush and water. Then decide how you wish to preserve the shell. If you intend to keep them in your own collection, the amount of cleaning you do is your own choice. But if you intend to sell or trade them, it is better to underclean a shell than to overclean it. Some shellers prefer to do the finishing themselves. The first step is to remove the animal, and that is no easy task. Bivalves are the easiest. Usually it is only necessary to leave them out of water for a few hours and they will open. Univalves are the most difficult to clean, and I usually take care of the small shells first. Tiny shells, which have very little meat in them, can be placed in a bottle of alcohol which dries the animal. Later the shells can be removed and preserved with the operculum (the trap door that serves both as a foot and a lid to protect the animal) still in place. A shell without the operculum is not considered complete and has little value.

"Larger shells present more of a problem. A good way to clean conch (*strombus*) is to place them in a container and ice them down for 48 hours. *Strombus* cannot live in cold water and icing it down kills the animal. Then, by using a jet of water and a little shaking, you can slide the animal right out. Shells with a high glaze should not be boiled because of the danger of clouding and spoiling the shell's finish. Common shells can be cleaned by boiling if it is done properly. Place the shell in cold water and bring it slowly to a boil. Continue to simmer gently, the length of time depending upon the size of the animal. A few minutes will take care of a small rock shell, but a large horse conch (*Pleuroploca gigantea*) will take as long as one-half hour. Some people prefer to rot out the animal. This is a long, drawn-out method which must be watched carefully. The procedure is to place the shell in a pan of water and allow it to disintegrate. Each day the water must be changed and the animal parts washed out until the shell is completely free of odor and meat. It is recommended that the jar be placed outside the house, as far away as possible, or the odor may cause you to give up shell collecting. A shell can be ruined by leaving it too long in water fouled with decayed animal parts. The acid from the decayed flesh attacks the shell and destroys the finish. To have a good collector's item, a shell should be perfect in every way. The operculum should be saved, and when the shell is ready, it should be replaced in the shell. One method is to stuff the shell with cotton and then cement the operculum in place with a small amount of rubber cement.

"Marine growth and coral deposits on shells can be removed by soaking them in a solution of bleach and water. Do not allow them to remain in the water too long, or you will overclean and spoil the luster. Do not use muriatic acid as it will attack the shell as well as the growth you are trying to remove. The color of a finished product can be brought out by oiling with a solution of one part baby oil to two parts lighter fluid. Remember that a shell is the home of a small creature, built with infinite care. If cleaned properly, it will be a source of enjoyment and beauty for many years.

"If you ship shells home from a vacation, packing them properly to prevent damage is just as important as the cleaning process. Many a shell collector has spent hours hunting for choice specimens and additional hours cleaning and preserving them, only to have his work ruined by improper or careless packing. All shells should be considered fragile and each should be packed in a separate box or container stuffed with shredded newspaper or similar material. Do not use cotton as it tends to adhere to the spines and projections of the shell and is difficult to remove. Popcorn is excellent. It is light, so it doesn't add much weight to the package, is soft so it doesn't damage the most fragile shell, and it forms around irregular shapes to prevent shifting and bumping. Separately boxed shells can be placed in a sturdy carton, and shipped as one package. But keep the weight and size of each carton small so that freight handlers can load and unload it easily. Large, heavy packages are apt to receive rougher treatment than smaller ones that are more easily handled."

By adding a knowledge of shells and shell collecting procedures to your underwater hunting skills, a whole new wonderful world of sea shells will be opened for you and your diving will be rewarded by a beautiful, permanent collection of King Neptune's special jewelry.

Inhabiting the nooks and crannies of submerged reefs are "ugly crawling things" which are fun to catch and delicious to eat. Joyce Irwin displays a lobster taken while free diving off Isla Mujeres, Yucatán. (*Photo by Mick Church*)

6 *Those Ugly Crawling Things*

SEARCHING the nooks and crannies of submerged reefs will bring
you into contact with animals which are much faster and better able to
defend themselves than shellfish. In the same hiding places you will
meet ferocious-appearing creatures with spindly legs, sharp spines
and grotesque bodies which often cause them to be dubbed "those
ugly crawling things." These are the sea worms, sea slugs, sea spiders,
crabs, lobsters and octopuses which, in spite of their vicious appearance, can be hunted and captured with no other weapon than your
bare hands. Sea worms and sea slugs are harmless creatures which are
usually ignored because they have no food value. Sea spiders are large
crablike animals with tremendously long legs and small bodies. They
are grayish-white in color and when seen crawling awkwardly over
the rocks, their grotesque bodies look like something out of a night-
mare. They are very slow moving and can be easily captured by hand.
The only precaution is to wear gloves to protect your hands from its
spines. Also keep your hands away from its tiny mouth and the pin-

cers at the end of two of its legs. The best way is to come from behind
and grab its body toward the back. Or you can use both hands to
hold the legs that are armed with pincers. Most people do not consider spider crabs edible, but I have a suspicion that the animal's un-
appetizing appearance is responsible for their aversion. When boiled
in sea water, the meat of the legs has a delicious flavor, but it is rich
and a small portion usually satisfies most people.

Most large crabs can move much faster than sea spiders, and could
probably escape a skin diver if they weren't so pugnacious. They depend upon their claws for protection and usually if touched or teased,
they raise their claws over their heads and challenge you to a battle.
The claws cannot reach the top of their shell and you can safely grab
them by the body as long as your fingers do not slip to the underside.
But don't underestimate the speed with which a pugnacious crab can
turn around. Many a diver has returned to shore nursing a bruised
finger because his hand moved too slowly when he made his grab.
Another good method is to grab a claw in each hand. The pincers
only have power when crushing and are helpless when held closed.
But be sure you catch both claws at the same time. If you miss with
one hand, the crab will get you with its free claw. Also, since both
hands are occupied with crab claws, getting it into your goody bag
can present a major problem. If you need a free hand to open your
bag, it's time to call for a buddy, swim to the boat or to shore, or develop the finger dexterity of a magician. This is why the type of bag
you use and the way you use it is important.

Free divers working from shore, or at any time when not directly
under a boat, should always use a surface float. The float not only
comes in handy as a rest platform between dives, but by tying a bag
and extra equipment to it, you save yourself a long swim every time
you bring something up from the bottom. The float can be almost
anything as long as it gives you something to hold to and will float
the weight of your catch. However, towing a float with a heavy sack
dangling down into the water will slow your progress, especially if
you are working in kelp and weeds. Many divers tie the mouth of a
sack around the inside of an inner tube so it stays open while the tube
is floating on the surface. This is more streamlined than a bag dangling from a rope, and objects placed inside the inner tube drop into

the open mouth of the bag. If the inner tube is also equipped with a lid, live specimens can't swim back out. Surf mats or a paddleboard make ideal surface floats, because they provide a platform which will carry a sackful of specimens out of the water. Throw your catch on top and you can move much faster over the surface. Most divers prefer a sack with a wire mouth that opens like a woman's purse. These are called "bug" bags, and can be purchased at all dive shops. If you have ever tried to put a spiny, wiggling sea creature into a loose gunnysack in the water, you will appreciate their value. I have watched scuba divers burn up a whole tank of air while trying to accomplish this feat underwater. The procedure is almost as difficult while treading water on the surface. The animal's legs and spines can get so thoroughly tangled up in the fibers of the bag that it's difficult to unwind them even on shore. A pursetype opens like a net when moved through the water and gives you a chance to get your catch inside before it gets tangled in the material. When diving with scuba, a nylonmesh bug bag can be rolled up and tucked into your weight belt where it is out of the way until you need it.

One of the most challenging and rewarding of all skin-diving activities is hunting lobsters (or "bugs" as they are called in diver terminology). These delicious crustaceans are found in temperate waters throughout the world. All are excellent eating, and all bring a high price in restaurants and fish markets. However, many people are shocked to learn that the familiar lobsters with the great claws are found only along the Northeast-Atlantic coast of America. The rest of the world's lobsters have spines and feelers, but no claws. With or without claws, lobsters are hunted by skin divers in much the same fashion as for other bottom-dwelling creatures. However, grabbing lobsters with claws requires an entirely different technique from that used for spiny lobsters.

Allan R. Boehm, writing in *Skin Diver* magazine, October, 1967, gives an excellent description of the technique for hunting large New England lobsters. Allan says, "In the Long Island, New York area we have numerous wrecks, many of which were depth charged after sinking, to minimize hazards to the shipping lanes of busy New York port. These wrecks are the prime areas for the exciting art of gathering bugs by hand. The tools of the trade are few—a twenty-foot length of $\frac{3}{16}$-inch nylon cord, a quick sure grip in your hands and, last but not least, cool calculating nerve. Large lobsters, seven pounds and up, can be found on wrecks in a depth of 100 feet or more all year round. For this reason, bug diving is not limited to any one season of the year.

"The *San Diego* is an excellent bug-hunting wreck as it lies in a capsized position with much of the superstructure forming hiding spots. Make your descent directly to the ocean floor and start a methodical search. Since the light at this point is usually quite dim, progress is slow and movement should be kept to a minimum to keep from stirring up the bottom. You'll observe the first telltale signs— marks in the sand leading into a crevice, and whiplike antennae protruding ominously from the hole. With his presence now certain, the most important facts to ascertain are his approximate size and the exact position of the crusher claw. Here, I might point out that the position of the crusher claw is not a constant factor. Therefore, on each individual lobster you must be certain if this claw is on his right or left side. This can easily be determined by peering into the hole and carefully observing the claws. White, toothlike mounds lining the inside edge of the pincer, and its extremely large girth, quickly identify the crusher claw. In comparison, the other cutting claw is much narrower in girth and very pointed at the tip. There is no white coloration on this claw whatsoever.

"Having determined the weight at about thirteen pounds, and the crusher claw on his right side, swift action is now called for. Bait him with your right hand to draw his first defensive move, which is usually to attack the dangling fingers with his crusher claw. At this point, deliberate and precise judgement must be executed. Grab the outside edge of the crusher claw and pull it to your left. Your right hand simultaneously moves for the outside edge of the cutting claw, which has already started moving to free the crusher claw. With both claws secure in your hands and spread as far apart as possible, exert a steady pressure with a slight rotating movement to free the captive from his den.

"It must be noted here that hesitation, miscalculation or not getting a secure grip on the claws can result in a badly bruised hand, broken fingers and, with extremely large lobsters, a fractured wrist.

If you have ever tried to put a spiny, wiggling sea creature into a bag under-water, you will appreciate the value of a pursetype "bug bag." Author, Bill Barada, prepares to bag a 14-pound lobster taken off Southern California's Cortes Bank. (*Photo by Paul Tzimoulis*)

If you should be unfortunate enough to be grabbed by a large bug, a quick clockwise or counterclockwise rotation of the arm can minimize the extent of injury. This action will dismember the claw from your captor. The loss of a claw will not cripple a lobster permanently as they grow new ones.

"Having successfully removed your prize from his home, secure him to a nylon line with a clove hitch around his tail portion. Then turn him loose on the sandy area adjacent to the wreckage. His tendency will be to move away from you, and as long as you keep your body between him and the wreckage you will have little trouble with him trying to escape by re-entering the wreck."

Allan didn't say how you tied a clove hitch around its tail while holding the claws with both hands. This is somewhat like the situation with the crab, described earlier, and I assume it's one of the times when a diving buddy comes in mighty handy.

"The search is continued, and once a second bug is captured and secured to the line, approximately a lobster length apart, your problems are minimized. Bugs tied together will always move in opposite directions, therefore, placed eight to ten feet off the wreckage, you can leave them for short periods of time unattended. The more bugs attached to the line, the less movement takes place. However, they have a tendency to reach out and grasp at passing objects, so I would suggest you use caution when passing fellow divers.

"In closing, I will point out that lobsters migrate into shallow areas in summer months. At this time they can be found under large rocks and in rough-bottom areas in five to ten feet of water. Inlet jetties and bridge abutments are another excellent source of supply. My largest lobster, 21 pounds, was taken in 60 feet of water in summer months. It is not uncommon to take as many as eight, 10- to 15-pound lobsters off a single wreck in one day during the peak migratory time. I would also like to mention that the bug bag (goody bag) is still the most efficient way to gather small lobsters. And I suggest that before going in quest of large bugs, practice by handling small ones."

Bob White, a diving instructor in Beverly, Massachusetts says, "Many beginners overlook lobsters simply by swimming too fast. I have found them hiding under a single piece of seaweed that almost

Ed Malinewski with a 14-pound lobster taken in a wreck off Barnegat Inlet, New Jersey. (*Photo by Paul Tzimoulis*)

covered their body. I believe that the early-morning hours are best for hunting lobsters, not early afternoon, and more of them will be in the open on a rainy or overcast day than when the sun is bright. The best time of year is in the middle of summer when the lobsters move into shallow water. In the early part of the season a diver should pay close attention to the temperature; sometimes just hunting for a shallow, warmer spot will uncover a colony."

Bob also recommends the use of a probe, not for spearing lobsters, but to herd them into the open, or to investigate seaweed-covered holes without exposing your hand to a lurking eel. He says a good place to look for lobsters is beneath a reddish-brown seaweed that covers the rocks like a carpet of moss. Bob uses a probe to feel through the moss, or lift it aside to disclose lobsters feeding beneath it. His pet complaint is against divers who do not carry a gauge to measure their size while still underwater. These divers place shorts in their bag along with legal-size bugs to measure them after they get to shore. The larger lobsters fight and kill many of the small ones, and half of the shorts returned to the water are already dead. Bob believes that lobsters shed their claws too easily to depend upon this method of grabbing them. He says it's better and safer to grab them by the body.

Frank Scalli and Will LeFavre introduced me to New England lobster hunting one summer off Gloucester. It was a day when the stormy Atlantic lay calm and peaceful, and we found clear water in a shallow cove surrounded by the rocky grandeur of the New England shoreline. The flat bottom was a mixture of sand and rocks which were covered with vegetation and marine growth. It was practically crawling with lobsters. We found them nestled and half-buried in the sand next to the rocks, sitting in crevices and slots, hiding under patches of seaweed and out in the open crawling over the bottom. The lobsters lay with their great claws folded across the front of their bodies and always faced the opening to a hole. Frank had warned me, "Watch out for the claws. Grab them from the back and don't

Warren Wells (left), Chief Engineer for Bendix Pacific, is an avid "bug" diver as evidenced by this catch he and some companions made off Southern California's Cortes Bank. (*Photo by Paul Tzimoulis*)

let your fingers get underneath where the claws can reach them." It sounded a lot like crab hunting. I did fine as long as they were in the open, where I could tease them into an attack so I could grab the claws. But those wedged into a narrow slot gave me trouble. Frank failed to tell me how I was supposed to get my hand in back of a lobster that refused to co-operate. He was having no trouble. Time after time I watched him put his hand straight in over the top of a tightly wedged lobster, dig it out of the hole, and come off scot free. When questioned about it later his answers were evasive. All I could get were comments such as, "It's a trick you learn after a while— You've got to be quick—I hypnotize them so they don't pinch." He was right about one thing. You do have to be quick. His "trick" is that the claws of small lobsters do not have enough span to grasp the forearm of a skin diver which is protected by thick wet-suit material. As long as his fingers and hand got safely past the claws, he could grab the lobster and pull it out of the hole.

The spiny lobster of the West Coast is much faster and less pugnacious than his New England cousin. When threatened, the New England lobster will raise its claws and challenge you to battle rather than try to escape. Catching one is simply a matter of outmaneuvering the claws. Catching a West Coast lobster is somewhat like trying to catch a fly. Its long, whiplike feelers are as sensitive as radar, and the slightest threat or quick movement will send it scuttling far back into the rocks, usually well out of reach. They sit in the entrances of holes, their feelers searching the water for the approach of food or enemies. Often an entire colony, or family, will inhabit the same crevice, and a forest of feelers will be seen protruding from every rock. The trick is to get your hand past the feelers and obtain a firm grip on its body before the lobster scuttles into the hole. Grabbing the feelers is useless. The lobster sheds them as easily as a lizard sheds its tail. If you approach with arms outstretched, the lobster will back away before you can reach it. Move in with your hands held wide and back, even with your face. Wait until you are very close, then aim for a spot about six inches behind its tail. They are so fast that a quick grab for the head will catch nothing but water.

The holes are usually infested with sea urchins and are often too small for your hand to reach past the lobster. In this case, they can sometimes be caught by feinting the feelers away from one of your hands. The lobster is almost blind and "sees" through its feelers. Move very slowly and try to get one feeler guarding your face mask and the other on one of your hands. A quick grab with the hand on his "blind" side will sometimes net you the lobster. In shallow holes, with no back or side entrances, you can sometimes reach a lobster after it has scuttled. But, you can pull your heart out and the lobster will never budge unless you know the trick that will break his grip. The tough, sharp spines of a lobster slant forward, and once it is wedged into a hole and braces its legs, pulling it out is like pulling a foxtail or burr backward through a sweater. The harder you pull, the tighter the bug wedges into the rocks. But if you shake it violently, forward and backward, it becomes confused and can easily be pulled out. One explanation is that the lobster's equilibrium is controlled by a disc inside its head which is filled with a few grains of sand. Shaking the lobster is supposed to cause the sand to swirl inside the disc and makes the lobster so dizzy it becomes helpless. The theory is embellished by a story of a scientific experiment in which iron filings were substituted for sand inside the disc. When a magnet was held above the lobster's head, the iron filings were pulled upward and the lobster turned upside down. This is said to be the reason that shaking a lobster will break its grip on the rocks.

The Pacific coast lobster, found from central California south into Mexico, grows to a tremendous size. Almost half of the weight of a New England lobster is in its giant claws. The weight of a spiny lobster is all body and legs. For this reason a 20-pound spiny lobster has a much larger body than its New England counterpart of the same weight. I have taken many spiny lobsters which weighed more than 20 pounds. Their huge bodies measured almost two feet from head to tail and their backs were so broad, I could barely span them with two hands. The legs were about two inches in diameter and had a spread of more than three feet. Underwater, the size of everything you see is magnified approximately one fourth, and meeting one of these monsters face to face inside a cave can be an unnerving experience to the uninitiated. An old-time diving friend will never forgive me for an incident that occurred because I forgot how terrifying a really big lobster can be under the right circumstances.

We were diving off Refugio Beach, California, and the water was so dirty our hands disappeared when we extended our arms. This is often good for bug diving because they aren't so nervous and, when you do see a lobster, it is so close all you need to do is grab. But murky-water diving in the kelp gives an eerie sensation at best until you become accustomed to it. And suddenly sighting a big bug a few inches from your eyes in the gloom of an underwater cave has shaken up many an experienced diver. My friend had never seen a giant lobster underwater and, when I bumped into a real monster, I decided to let him catch it. I told him to follow me down and I would point to the bug so he could find it. I dived to the bottom, caught hold of a rock next to the lobster's hole and pointed. My friend held back, too far for his eyes to adjust to the dimness inside the cave and too far for him to be able to see the bug. Anxious to help, I grabbed his shoulder and yanked, guiding his head into the hole. His reaction was instantaneous. I felt him struggle frantically. My mask was knocked off. The wind was kicked out of me. And I sensed a blur of scrambling arms, legs and flippers as my companion shot for the surface.

In my determination to "help" my friend, I had forgotten that huge

The author demonstrates a technique for bagging his lobsters. If held by the horns, and sacked in a single, swift motion, the bug's legs fold along its body and do not grab the sack. (*Photo by Paul Tzimoulis*)

bulls often advance threateningly toward an intruder. My friend said he saw an apparition that looked like a monstrous, prehistoric dragon advancing menacingly a few inches from his face. And I was holding his head so he couldn't escape.

The spiny lobsters of tropical coral reefs are smaller than Pacific coast lobsters. Their legs are longer and they have sharper spines. In fact, almost everything that grows or lives in coral seems to be honed to a finer edge than those of rocky reefs. The coral itself is razor sharp, sea-urchin spines are longer and more penetrating, and many of the fish have fins that can puncture a leather glove. Digging spiny bugs out of a coral reef requires much the same finesse as for Pacific coast lobsters, but use extra caution to keep from being badly cut by coral or punctured by sea-urchin spines. I learned this lesson the hard way the first time I went after bugs in the Florida Keys. The water was a warm 85 degrees and my only protection was a bathing suit and thin, canvas gloves. I went after a colony of lobsters in the slam-bang style of the Pacific coast where a full wet suit prevents injury from most marine life. I caught the lobsters, but my arms and legs were lacerated with coral cuts and decorated with sea-urchin spines. After that I wore a sweat shirt, leather gloves and used a more delicate finesse.

A characteristic of tropical lobsters which I have never observed on the Pacific coast is that occasionally they appear stunned or dazed and can be picked up as easily as rocks on the bottom. The first time I noticed this phenomena was at Tiburon Island in the Gulf of California, Mexico. A sudden upwelling had reduced the water temperature from a warm 80 degrees to a frigid 50 degrees, and the bugs were so sluggish that they seemed unable to move. Catching them was simply a matter of reaching out and picking them up. I attributed our good luck to the sudden drop in temperature. But later I encountered this phenomena in the Caribbean when the water was very warm. Lobsters chased into the open, appeared to be stunned or confused and made little attempt to escape. Now, when lobster hunting in the tropics, I use the shaft of a spear gun or similar probe to frighten them out of their holes. Once they are in the open, these bugs are often easily caught.

A creature which cannot be chased out of its hole without the use

The spiny lobsters of tropical coral reefs are smaller than Pacific coast lobsters. Jenny Caperton bags a nice one in 60 feet of water off Cozumel Island, Mexico. (*Photo by Mick Church*)

of chemicals is the octopus. There are hundreds of varieties inhabiting almost all the waters of the world, but the giant octopus, which
is the vicious villain of fiction stories, exists only in the cold waters of
the Pacific Northwest. In other parts of the world a large octopus has
tentacles that measure no more than five feet from tip to tip across
its body. Between northern Canada and Point Conception, California are monsters that weigh well over 100 pounds with tentacles
that measure more than 20 feet from tip to tip. The largest octopus
ever recorded was taken from Puget Sound and had a tentacle spread
of 36 feet.

The octopus is a bottom-crawling creature that hides in the reefs by
day and comes out at night to feed on crabs, clams and other shellfish.

Tangling with the giant octopus of the Pacific Northwest, compared to small
ones in other waters, is similar to graduating from pussycats to mountain lions.
Dale Dean, of the Puget Sound Mudsharks Club, faces a 60-pound, 12-foot-
long giant, 120 feet beneath the surface. (*Photo by William L. High*)

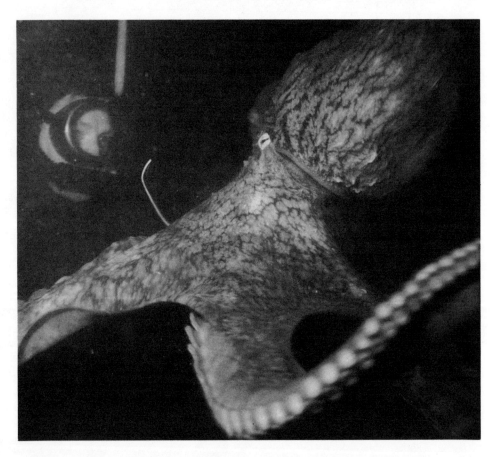

They are poor swimmers and a skin diver can play with small ones almost like a pet. They have a beak similar to a parrot and some try to bite. But the wound is usually no more severe than the peck of a bird. Most of the time they are too frightened to bite. The only danger is from a species of the South Pacific that injects a poison with its beak which can make you seriously ill. Usually a pair of heavy gloves is ample protection and small octopuses can be handled safely by novice skin divers. But tangling with the giants of the Pacific Northwest is graduating from pussycats to mountain lions.

For many years the giant octopus was an unknown threat, and we all wondered what would happen if a diver prowling the caves of a reef accidentally bumped into a really big one. Then we heard that Puget Sound divers were actually hunting these monsters and capturing them with their bare hands. On my next vacation I headed for Puget Sound with a movie camera to capture this epic battle on film.

My instructors in the gentle art of octopus wrestling were Gary Keffler, Dale Dean and Ed Thomas of the Puget Sound Mudsharks Club. Our first dive was at a place called Blakeley Rock, a small island a few miles off Seattle. The water was quite clear, and I had a ringside view of the proceedings after Gary spotted an octopus. Gary invited me to "take a look" and following his directions, I peered into the hole and saw a large red blob of pulsating flesh, topped by two small eyes that stared at me hypnotically. Surrounding its body were double rows of white suction discs that lined the inside of whiplike tentacles. As I watched, the tentacles began slowly writhing and twisting. It gave me an uneasy feeling and I backed out.

I asked Gary what happened when a diver grabbed an octopus in its lair. For an answer he dived to the rocks, grabbed the octopus and pulled with all his might. The octopus clung tightly to the rocks until Gary's grip slipped and it snapped back into the hole. Then Gary invited me to try. I grabbed the octopus with both hands and pulled. It was like trying to hang onto a handful of grease with muscles. The octopus stretched like a rubber band and the harder I pulled, the tighter it clung to the rocks. And the tighter I squeezed, the faster it squirted out of my hands. It broke free and snapped back to its original position. Not a single tentacle or suction disc had attached to my body.

The Mudsharks said an octopus attacked in its den never tried to hold the diver. They also explained that it is almost impossible to pull a big one out of its hole. They use salt to drive the octopus out in the open. A double handful of salt dumped in front of the hole and fanned toward the octopus irritates its gills and forces it to leave its den.

I hovered above and watched as Gary salted the hole. Nothing happened for a few minutes. Then huge tentacles began snaking out from under the rock, writhing and darting in all directions as if seeking an adversary. Finally, a huge cloud of dust boiled from the opening and the great blob of its body lumbered into the open. Gary pounced, grabbing the octopus by the body and jerking it off the bottom in one quick motion. I fully expected to see the octopus tentacles surround Gary in the classic death grip so often depicted by artists. But apparently Gary's biggest problem was hanging onto his slippery opponent, which was only struggling to get away. Gary swam easily to shore and deposited his catch on the beach. Then said, "Now, let's go find yours."

I learned that octopuses do fight back when you grab them. I followed Gary's procedure, grabbed the body with both hands, jerked it off the rocks, and found myself struggling with a squirming, slippery sea monster. It was like trying to keep a grip on a handful of eels. I had to continually change my grip to prevent its escape. The tenacles lashed wildly in all directions, attaching to anything that got in their way. One caught my face mask and pulled it to one side so it filled with water. Another caught my air hose and I almost lost my mouthpiece. I clamped down with my teeth, but the tentacle continued to tug and my jaws ached with the effort to hold it in my mouth. A tentacle caught one leg, another my head and they drew me into a jackknife so that I was swimming with one flipper. When I finally reached shore, both the octopus and I were thoroughly exhausted. Ed Thomas swam up, inspected my catch and commented sympathetically, "Too bad, Bill. It's only a baby ten-footer. Turn it loose and let's go find its daddy."

Ed wasn't joking. We hunted octopuses from Tacoma to Vancouver, in harbors, piers, ferry docks, wrecks and reefs. We found them hiding in sewer pipes, hollow logs, in the piling of piers and docks,

Jo Ann Duffy displays the 45-pound octopus with which she won the Woman's 1966 Octopus Wrestling Championship in Puget Sound, Washington. This is an annual event which draws divers from all over the Pacific Northwest. (*Photo by Gary Rubottom*)

and one big one had its home in an old pot-bellied stove someone had thrown overboard. Each hiding place was marked by a ring of dead crab and clam shells stacked around the outside of the den like a miniature breakwater or fortress. Most were in shallow water, but one monster, caught at a depth of 80 feet, wrapped itself around Gary's legs and almost immobilized his flippers. I got some wonderful footage before Ed Thomas swam in and helped to break its grip. When we got it to the surface, it measured out at 18 feet.

Skin divers hunt giant octopuses primarily for the sport of wrestling them. Usually the defeated octopus is released and it returns to

Fisheries biologist, William L. High, after winning an underwater wrestling match with a 42-pound octopus. Mr. High, a recognized authority, has been studying octopus habits for a decade. (*Photo by Bud Abbey*)

the same den where it can be caught again another day. A few are kept for food and, when properly prepared, the meat is delicious. It is somewhat tough and rubbery and has a texture similar to an over-boiled lobster. The flavor is also similar to crab or lobster and, if shredded into a cocktail or salad, few people could tell the difference.

Scientifically the octopus is a mollusk, or shellfish, with the shell (beak) on the inside of its body rather than the outside. It is also nocturnal, hiding by day and feeding at night, and divers hunting at night often see them out in the open, crawling over the bottom in search of other shellfish.

After the sun goes down, the submarine world takes on an entirely different appearance and a diver with an underwater light will see things that never appear during daylight. Nocturnal creatures that bury themselves deep inside a reef and in the sand come out at night and stalk the ocean floor in search of prey. Rare and beautiful sea shells, which must be traced and hunted by day, are out in the open where they can be picked up by the rays of an underwater light, their colors flashing a signal of their location. Clams, crabs, lobsters and all of the night-crawling creatures are more easily hunted and caught by diving after dark. In the beam of a powerful light you will see the reef dressed in colors more brilliant than in daytime as the animals and organisms put on their most festive evening clothes. Coral polyps, sea worms, tunicates and other organisms blossom with delicately colored tendrils. Sea shells and shellfish spread lacy plumage, and lobsters appear as red as if fresh from the boiling pot. Many of the fish change colors and almost all creatures are hypnotized by the rays of a light. Lobsters caught in the beam will freeze motionless until you touch them, and lobster hunting at night is a little like jacklighting for rabbits with the beam of automobile headlights. Even fish are hypnotized and those that are usually wary and spooky can be caught and played with by hand. Many fish sleep at night, resting on the sand or nestled in the nooks and chinks of a reef. The parrot fish covers itself with a blanket of membranous tissue like a cocoon. These fish are so confused by the beam of a light, or are so drugged with sleep, that they make no attempt to escape and you can actually hold them and pet them.

The dangers of night diving are a little different, but no greater, than those in the daytime. The greatest difference is a lack of range in visibility, both underwater and on the surface. If there is a bright moon in a cloudless sky, the clear waters of a tropical coral reef permit visibility without a light. But on a dark night, or when overcast, your range of vision is limited to the cone of artificial light. A good precaution when diving from a boat is to place powerful lights on the boat that shine both down into the water and into the air. Surfacing on a dark night, out of sight of land or a boat, is like surfacing in the middle of the ocean, and it is sometimes difficult to know in which direction to swim.

But, if you have never tried it, don't pass up an opportunity to dive on a tropical coral reef at night. It will be an experience you will never forget, and one you won't regret.

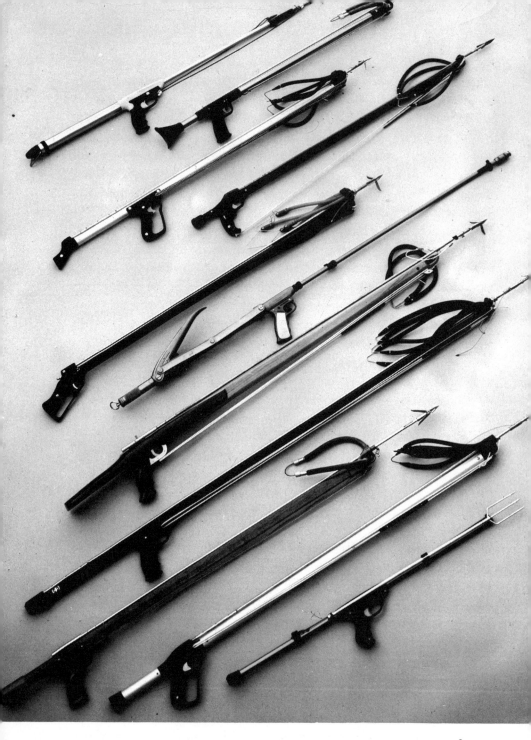

The arsenal of weapons confronting an underwater hunter often puzzles experienced divers, and is completely baffling to the novice. (*Photo by* Skin Diver *magazine*)

theories behind the various types and their advantages and disadvantages will help you select the ones best suited to your needs.

The first spearfishing weapon used by skin divers was the hand spear, or pole spear, and it is still very efficient for the diver who knows how to use it. I still carry a hand spear on my float and, when the water is very dirty, or the fish are holed up in rocks and caves, I prefer it to a spear gun. The reason is, its simplicity of operation, its effectiveness for close-range work on small fish, and the fact that you often get in two or three shots on a single dive. My original weapon was a broomstick armed with a five-tine "frog gig." For a short time this weapon was used without rubber slings or other means of propulsion, and I tried to spear fish underwater by jabbing at them by hand. This was my first experience with the effect of the density of water on fast moving objects, which is the controlling factor in the performance of all underwater weapons. No matter how hard I tried or how much force I used, the spear moved through the water so slowly that the fish dodged it easily. When I was lucky enough to hit an unwary target, the impact was so gentle that the fish bounced off uninjured except for the loss of a few scales. Even when the five tines were exchanged for a single, needle-sharp barb, impaling a free-swimming fish was a matter of luck and timing. By holding to the rocks with my free hand, and pulling myself forward as I jabbed with the spear, I managed to land a few by pinning them against the rocks. But the fish had all of the advantages and I was no threat to their existence until more effective methods were developed.

The addition of a rubber sling, or loop, to the butt end of the hand spear increased its effectiveness tremendously. The spear is cocked by placing your hand in the sling and stretching the rubbers along the shaft. Grasp the spear shaft with the hand holding the rubbers and keep them stretched until ready to fire. Jab as you release your grip and the rubbers will shoot the spear forward. The distance the spear will travel, and how hard it will hit, depends upon both the strength of the rubbers and the distance they are stretched. A resilient gum rubber, with at least a four-to-one stretch, makes the best propellent. Synthetic rubber, such as neoprene, does not have the resiliency or recovery characteristics of gum rubber and should not be used. Surgical tubing is an ideal propellent, not only because of the material, but because the hole through the tubing permits the outside walls to compress without resistance and the rubber can be stretched farther. Solid tubing, or solid rubber, compresses into a hard inner core which limits the distance it can be stretched. Don't select rubbers that are either too strong or too light. A set of light rubbers will drive your spear its full range, but the speed and impact will not be sufficient to impale a fish. A set of heavy rubbers will give speed and impact but, if you can't stretch them to their full capacity, the range will be reduced. Use the strongest rubbers that you can stretch three times the length of the loop. A heavy cord wrapped around the shaft to form a handgrip will help keep the spear from slipping after it is cocked. The length of the spear is governed by the same rules as all underwater weapons. One diver I know uses a 14-foot spear to hunt white sea bass and yellowtail in open water. This length would be useless in rocks and kelp where a seven- or eight-foot spear is needed. On an eight-foot spear I use a two-foot loop that I can stretch to six feet. When the spear is cocked, my hand is within two feet of the spearhead. This gives easy handling in close quarters and sufficient range to impale a fish three or four feet away. If the pull of the rubbers tends to bend the shaft, twist it once or twice to equalize the tension. The spear should be designed to float point downward in the water. If it floats flat, it is too light and you will be fighting to get it headed in the right direction. For rock fishing, I like a heavy four- or five-tine spearhead that can be slammed into the reef without bending out of shape. When a fish is hit with this head, drive forward with your flippers until it is pinned against a rock, then slide down the shaft and get hold of it with your hands. This technique will capture partially missed fish that would otherwise escape.

Modern factory-made hand spears are a far cry from my crude, homemade weapon. The best ones are tapered like a fishing rod to give less resistance and added speed in the water. They are made of aluminum, fiberglass or stainless steel, are adjustable to almost any length, and have an assortment of spearheads to fit almost any situation. But the technique for using them is the same as the old style and their effectiveness still depends upon the ability of the diver.

The Hawaiian sling was the forerunner of modern spear guns originated for use in the clear waters of Hawaii and the Caribbean. It is a step between a hand spear and a spear gun, serving as an underwater version of the bow and arrow. The firing mechanism is a simple bamboo or metal tube with a rubber sling attached to one end. The rubber sling is equipped with an insert, or nock, to hold the end of a metal shaft, which is usually $\frac{5}{16}$ inch or $\frac{3}{8}$ inch in diameter and five or six feet long. The shaft is fired by holding the tubing with one hand and stretching the sling and spear as far back as possible with the other. It fires a free spear with no line attached, and Florida divers prowl the reefs with a spare sling around their necks and a quiver of extra spear shafts on their backs, much like bow hunters in the forest. Small and medium-sized fish impaled by a free spear swim erratically in circles and the weight of the shaft drags them to the bottom where they can be retrieved. Larger fish, such as grouper and snapper, will "hole up" after they are hit and the diver can follow them to plant a second or third shaft for the "kill" shot. Only a strong man with powerful arm and back muscles can get a lot of power and range out of a Hawaiian sling. Its disadvantages are that it requires both hands to fire, and accuracy is more a matter of instinct than aiming. Also, a free spear is almost useless in murky water or where the bottom is too deep. This is why the Hawaiian sling has never become popular on the Pacific and Atlantic coasts. I tried one in the Pacific and quickly lost three spears before I gave it up. One hit a fish that spun off into 150 feet of water before I could catch it. Another missed a fish and was lost in the jungle of vegetation on the bottom, and the third simply disappeared into the murk and I never saw it again. However, in the clear, shallow waters of the Caribbean, divers have made some fantastic catches with the sling. Grouper and jewfish weighing several hundred pounds have been taken and Arthur Pinder is reported to have killed a sailfish with one shot from a sling. But, for the average skin diver, the range of a sling is not much greater than a hand spear, and in most parts of the world some type of spear gun is more effective.

The basic types of spear guns are rubber, spring and pneumatic or gas powered. A few have been offered that use a cartridge but have never been accepted. Spring-powered guns are popular with European divers around the Mediterranean, but, for some reason, have never

The Hawaiian sling is an effective weapon in the hands of a diver who knows how to use it. (*Photo by Paul Tzimoulis*)

caught on with American divers. A long coiled spring inside the
barrel is compressed when the spear shaft is inserted. As with the
rubbers of a hand spear, the stronger the spring and the farther it
travels in contact with the shaft, the greater the range and power of
the gun. Some of the most powerful spring guns are almost seven
feet long and the springs are so strong that it requires a lot of strength
to cock them. The handle of most of these guns is located in the
center of the barrel and is carried with the rear half extending over
the diver's shoulder. This gives good balance to the gun, makes it
easy to handle in the water, and gives a lot more maneuverability
than long guns with the handle at one end. The shaft fired by a
spring does not have the speed of rubber- or gas-propelled shafts but
it is extremely accurate, and the heavier models will impale a large
fish at distances of fifteen feet. Its disadvantages are that the gun is
always cocked while the harpoon is in position, and it relies entirely
on a safety to prevent accidental firing. Also, the steel spring tends to
rust when used in salt water and will lose its efficiency unless cared
for meticulously. Rubber is also attacked by sun and salt water, but
the damage is more obvious and the rubbers are more easily replaced.
Another disadvantage of spring guns is that sand or mud particles
inside the barrel create friction which reduces the efficiency of the
spring. Also, the range and power of these guns cannot be adjusted to
fit different situations. The length and strength of the spring is built
into each model and cannot easily be modified.

Gas guns were very popular for a while but quickly came into dis-
repute. They are banned in some areas and not allowed in most
spearfishing competitions. Most use compressed carbon dioxide as a
propellent, either in a small cylinder similar to a CO_2 fire extinguisher,
or in a cartridge similar to those for Seltzer bottles. The trigger re-
leases the gas or ruptures the cartridge, and the expanding gas drives
a shaft out of the barrel with terrific force. The advantage of these
guns is that their power does not depend upon the strength of the
diver and a child or a woman could fire the most powerful of them.
When properly designed, they have a tremendous range, driving a
heavy shaft through large fish at distances greater than twenty feet.
But their disadvantages more than offset their advantages. They are
extremely noisy, releasing a blast of bubbles with a sound like a mini-

ature explosion every time they are fired. The first shot from a CO_2 gun frightens every fish in the area. The cylinder type has a limited number of shots which are effective only as long as high pressure remains in the tank. Without a pressure gauge you never know when you are out of gas. This defect led me into a situation which resulted in my permanent disenchantment with CO_2 guns

The gun I was using was so powerful that when fired in the air, its ⅜-inch shaft would pull a 1000-pound test line, and split a 2×12-inch plank 100 feet away. In the water, its impact was so great that I was confident it would stop almost anything that swims. I was eager for a quarry worthy of this weapon and was looking for a fish big enough to test its power. The opportunity came while I was diving off Guaymas, Mexico. My target was a twelve-foot hammerhead shark approaching slowly along the reef. I grabbed the trusted CO_2 gun, descended to meet it head on, waited until it was at point-blank range about four feet away, and pulled the trigger. The gun sighed softly —the harpoon slid gently out of the barrel—and I stared helplessly at the shark with an empty gun in my hands. Fortunately, the shark was only mildly interested and swam quietly away. That was the last time I ever used a CO_2 gun. A leak had drained the pressure, rendering it useless.

CO_2 guns and pistols utilizing cartridges are just as bad as the cylinder type. The amount of pressure in individual cartridges varies widely, so you never know how much power you have when you pull the trigger. The cartridges can develop leaks which render them useless, and you can be hunting with an empty gun without realizing it. Firing mechanisms must release the gas instantly, and any corrosion or erratic performance destroys the gun's effectiveness. They make as much noise as the cylinder-type guns and, for this reason alone, a diver using a CO_2 gun will always be unpopular among a group of spearfishermen.

The principle of pneumatic guns is different from gas guns in that pressurized air never escapes to the water. Its only purpose is to drive a piston inside the barrel, which in turn drives the spear shaft. The diver pumps as much air into the cylinder as he wants, and the spear shaft cocks the gun by forcing the piston back against the pressure. The power of pneumatic guns is determined by the amount

Dick Barada, the author's son, and Carlos Ungson prowl the bottom off Cabo San Lucas, Mexico. An extension behind the gun handle makes it easier to maneuver and load in the water. (*Photo by Bill Barada*)

of pressure in the cylinder. Some models have a power adjustment which can be changed after the gun is cocked.

These guns are very powerful and quite accurate. The Brazilian spearfishing team won a world championship with pneumatic guns. However, the disadvantages are similar to those of spring guns. They are cocked all the time the shaft is in the barrel and rely on a safety to prevent accidents. Corrosion or sand inside the barrel is not as much a problem as with spring guns but the mechanism must be meticulously oiled and cleaned to keep it working smoothly. As with all guns which fire a harpoon from inside the barrel, a bent shaft or a substantial dent in the barrel renders them useless.

Rubber-powered guns are by far the most popular and the most versatile, and are universally accepted in all parts of the world. Hundreds of models are available from short, stubby versions two feet

long, to long-range weapons six feet in length. The shaft sits on top
of the barrel, held in place only at the muzzle and the end that
locks into the trigger mechanism, so problems of friction from the
barrel are eliminated. The gun can be carried with the harpoon in
place and is cocked only when the rubbers are loaded. Like hand
spears and sling guns, power is determined by the strength and resiliency of the rubber and the distance it is stretched. A long gun has
greater range and power than a short gun because rubber slings of the
same strength travel a greater distance in contact with the shaft. A
great advantage of rubber guns is that their power can be multiplied
simply by adding extra slings and even a short gun with double or
triple rubbers can develop amazing power and impact.

The length and weight of the spear shaft has a tremendous effect
upon the range, speed and impact of the gun you are using. If fired
from heavy rubber guns with identical power, a lightweight shaft of
$\frac{1}{4}$-inch or $\frac{5}{16}$-inch diameter will travel faster than a heavier shaft
of $\frac{3}{8}$-inch diameter. But the extra weight of the $\frac{3}{8}$-inch shaft gives
it more impact and penetrating power at a greater range. For this
reason, the lighter shafts should only be used with smaller guns
equipped with lightweight rubbers. For bigger guns used on larger
fish, a $\frac{3}{8}$-inch shaft will hit harder.

A good way to test the impact of different spear guns is to tie the
end of the harpoon line to a light spring scale and fire it underwater.
If you smear the face of the spring scale with colored grease, or similar substance, you will be able to measure the pull of the shaft when
it hits the end of the line. I have settled a lot of arguments as to the
merits of various guns with this simple test, and using a fish de-liar
as the spring scale.

When purchasing a rubber-powered gun, make sure that the rubbers stretch directly in line with the spear shaft. The end of the
shaft is free in the water the moment the trigger is pulled, and any
deviation tends to pull the shaft out of line. For several years, I used
a gun with the rubbers hooked to the muzzle an inch or so below
the shaft. Every time I fired, the rear of the shaft was pulled downward and the gun consistently shot high. In order to hit a fish, I had
to aim a few inches beneath it. The amount of compensation de-
pended upon how far it was away. I became so accustomed to this

compensation that when I finally got a gun that shot straight, I couldn't hit my hat. It took a lot of practice before I got back on target.

When selecting a powerful gun with multiple rubbers, make sure that the trigger will release easily under the tremendous tension. There are few things more frustrating than having a trigger "hang-up" when you have a prize fish in your sights. After a few immersions in salt water the levers inside the handle become rough and corroded, and some mechanisms that were designed for lighter-powered guns will not release under heavy tension. You should be able to squeeze off a shot with your spear gun as easily as when firing a rifle, and the trigger should have a minimum of travel before it fires. Many of your shots will be instinct shooting at fast-moving targets, and any trigger drag or delay will cause you to miss. If the trigger on a new gun is hard to pull or travels too far, you can bet it won't get any better after exposure to sun and salt water. Take your trigger apart regularly, clean the salt and corrosion out of it and coat all parts with silicone grease. It will last longer and give you the smooth operation that means fewer missed shots.

The position of the handle of a gun, whether at the end or toward the center of the barrel, is a subject of controversy among divers. Some prefer the ease of handling provided when the handle is positioned toward the center. Others like the extra reach they get when the full length of the gun extends beyond their hand. The weight of the gun should not be a factor in this decision, because in a high-quality gun, the barrel is sealed airtight so the gun will float when the shaft is removed, and it is as light as a feather in the water. I believe that with powerful guns, the ease of cocking the rubbers is more important than either the reach or maneuverability. On a gun designed so the rubbers must be stretched all the way to the end of the barrel, your arms and muscles will be in an awkward position, close to your body at the point of greatest tension. If the barrel extends eight to ten inches behind the last nock in the shaft, your arms have better leverage; you can pull harder and the rubbers are easier to load. An extension in back of the handle also gives better balance, because you can brace it against your forearm or under your armpit to help swing the gun sideways.

Al Schneppershoff with a 318-pound giant sea bass taken off Southern California. Al uses a big gun and a reel to hunt big fish. (*Photo courtesy of U. S. Divers Co.*)

Pinning a fish against the coral is a good way to prevent its escape. (*Photo by Mick Church*)

Using the right gun will help you hit your fish, but the method of rigging the line will determine whether you land it or not. Faulty, careless, or improper rigging will lose a fish just as quickly as poor marksmanship or using the wrong gun. The number of guns offered for sale with poorly designed rigging is amazing. Many manufacturers spend thousands of dollars designing and engineering an efficient, powerful weapon, but make no provision for rigging an adequate harpoon line. Some guns are equipped with such a mickey-mouse arrangement that it would take a magician to keep from getting it tangled or to restring it in the water. Often the line furnished with a gun is so weak and inadequate that a good-sized minnow would break it. Even on good guns, you will find a strong line tied carelessly to sharp projections or around sharp edges that cut it like a knife. When considering the purchase of a gun, inspect the method of rigging and releasing the line and keep these questions in mind: Does it have a positive line release that drops the line free in the water before the harpoon fires? Does the line holder have room for two or three loops of 250- to 300-pound test nylon line which is approximately ⅛ inch in diameter? How is the line fastened to the muzzle? Are there any sharp edges? Is the hole large enough to permit a new line to be attached easily? How is it attached to the slip ring on the spear shaft? Is the slip ring strong enough? Will it jam after a few months wear? How easily can the line be restrung while you are swimming in dirty water?

Any complications or projections that make it difficult should be avoided. Many times you will be loading your gun under awkward conditions and you should almost be able to do it blindfolded. The knots on a new gun are tied by factory workers on a production line and should all be retied. Nylon stretches when it is wet and ordinary overhand knots will come untied. Use a bowline and if you have room, put a double loop through metal holes. Burn the ends so they won't fray or unravel. Swivels, spring clips, and other hardware used on fishing lines will pull apart or break if used on a spear gun unless they are the extremely heavy-duty type used for harpooning broadbill swordfish.

Never underestimate the power of a big fish. Even medium-sized fish have tremendous speed and impact on their initial rush. I have watched a 25-pound yellowtail snap a 250-pound test line as if it were twine. The normal length of line is less than four times the length of the spear gun, between 15 and 20 feet. This is usually just enough to let the fish get up full speed, and it hits the end of the line with terrific force. If the line holds and the spearhead doesn't pull out, you will be dragged through the water and "go for a ride" until you, or the fish, become tired. Usually even a 300-pound test nylon line will not withstand the initial impact of a large fish, and divers hunting with scuba who want to "ride it out," use ³⁄₁₆-inch stainless steel cable. This is usually only practiced in water with a comparatively shallow bottom, or under special conditions such as the offshore rigs in the Gulf of Mexico. Free divers, or scuba divers working big fish in deep water, use a reel, breakaway rigging, or attach the line to a float so they can play the fish until it becomes tired.

The term "breakaway rigging" was coined to describe a method of attaching a long line to the shaft so that it will pay out only under the impact of a heavy fish. The line is attached to the spear shaft and coiled around the line release in the normal manner, but is not permanently tied to the muzzle. Instead, it is attached by a breakable line, usually 50- or 60-pound test fishing line, that will hold a small fish but will break when a heavy fish makes its initial rush. The balance of the line, usually 100 to 300 feet long, is coiled into a container clamped to the barrel of the gun. The end of this line is either attached to the gun or to an inflatable float. The end of the breakaway line can be rigged to inflate the float automatically or the float can be manually inflated.

With a breakaway, you can hunt small fish using only the usual amount of harpoon line. But if you hit a really big one, the breakaway absorbs the shock of its initial rush and the long line gives you a chance to reach the surface. The line pack must be rigged to pay out freely without tangles, and it must stay securely in place until it is needed. If your line pack comes loose while you are underwater, you may find yourself tangled in 200 feet of free-floating harpoon line.

Spear gun reels are used in the same manner as breakaway gear except that the reel replaces a container for holding the extra line. The normal length of line must be coiled around a line release and fired with the shaft because no reel, not even spinning reels, can pay out line as fast as the harpoon travels.

In some areas a surface float can be used to hold big fish. With this method, a rope or heavy line is tied from the spear gun to an inner tube or similar float on the surface which is towed behind the diver. In some cases, the line from the spear shaft is tied to the float, leaving the gun free after it is fired. In other cases, two lines are

Jack Prodanovich brings in a 35-pound roosterfish taken off Mulegé, Mexico in the Gulf of California. Note the line pack Jack uses with his breakaway. (*Photo courtesy of Voit Rubber Co.*)

fired with the shaft from the spear gun. One is attached in the normal fashion to the shaft, the other is attached to a detachable spearhead, which in turn is tied to the surface float.

Many divers prefer a two-line rigging to prevent loss of a spear shaft when hunting big fish. A normal length of line is attached to the shaft and permanently to the muzzle of the gun. The second line is the breakaway, or reel line, which is tied to a detachable spearhead. Both lines must be wound around the line release and fired with the harpoon. When a big fish is hit, only the line with the spearhead stays with the fish, while the shaft and gun pull free to be used again with another spearhead. An objection to using two lines is the problem of reloading and rerigging every time you fire. Handling two lines in the water can present some interesting tangles and can involve a lot of lost time. Using this system is a great incentive for care and accuracy with each shot. A few missed fish is a sure cure for careless shooting.

The correct spearhead, or barb, is just as important as the spear gun and rigging. Any spearhead, no matter what type, must be able to withstand the punishment of constant banging into rocks, coral and sand without breaking or bending so badly it becomes useless. It must also resist the corrosive effects of salt water and sunshine over long periods of time. Eating the flesh of a fish soiled by a rusty spearhead may pose a hazard to your health. Your spear gun is no stronger than its weakest link, so give a close inspection to all methods of attaching barbs, line, cable and tines to your spearhead. Look for sharp projections that will cut the line, loose or badly tied knots, weak or inadequate rivets and threaded joints, and flaws in welded or soldered joints. As with spear guns and rigging, the type of spearhead you should use will depend upon the kind of fish you are hunting, the terrain they inhabit and the clarity of the water. The barb that works perfectly on rockfish in dirty water will never hold a large, free-swimming fish in open water.

The three general categories of spearheads are: multitined, fixed heads and detachable heads. Multitined heads require less accuracy, will stand up under terrific banging into rocks and coral, and are more easily and quickly removed from the fish. They are most effective for hunting small fish around rocks and caves, and in dirty water

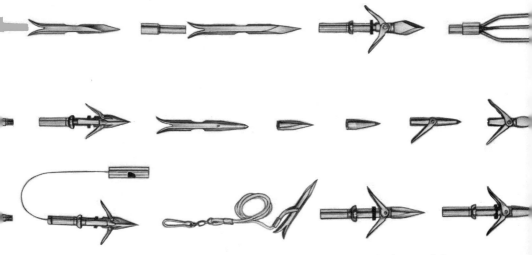

A variety of spearheads are available, ranging from stubby rock tips used for banging into coral, to razor-sharp tri-cut points that slice their way through a fish. (*Photo courtesy of Voit Rubber Co.*)

where snap shooting is often necessary. Heavy tines, with a minimum diameter of $\frac{3}{16}$ inch, are a must. Otherwise, the spearhead will be bent into a pretzel by the first decent-sized fish you hit.

Fixed single-point heads are usually screwed to the shaft, and depend upon either double or single-swinging barbs to hold the fish. They have greater penetrating power and will take larger fish at a greater range than multitined heads. The barbs fold back along the shaft as the head penetrates the fish, then spring outward to prevent its escape. A clip is provided to hold the barbs in place so the fish can be removed. If the shaft does not completely penetrate the fish, this clip often slides over the barbs, prevents them from swinging open and the shaft pulls out. Bending the tip of the barbs outward with a pair of pliers will prevent this from happening. Another source of trouble is the threads holding the head to the shaft. It is amazing how many manufacturers design these threads so the spearhead cannot be locked securely, with the result that a spinning fish or harpoon unscrews the head from the shaft. On many models, the only way to prevent the spearhead from unscrewing is to deliberately damage the threads or seal them with cement.

A variety of spear points are available for fixed heads, ranging

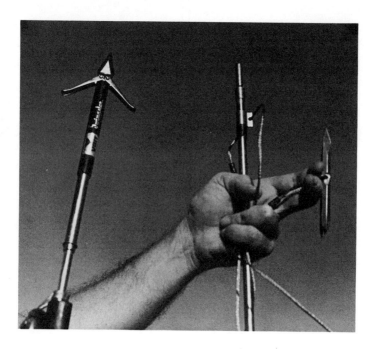

Swinging-barb spearheads, left, punch a larger hole and have less holding power than a straight slip tip, right. (*Photo by Bill Barada*)

from stubby, rock tips used for banging into coral, to razor-sharp tri-cut points that slice their way through a fish. A razor-sharp cutting tip is fine for open water, but worthless in rocks and coral unless it is tough enough to hold its edge. Drop the spear shaft, point downward, on a cement sidewalk and you will quickly see what will happen when it is fired into a rock from a powerful spear gun.

A large fish can bend a heavy shaft so badly that it is rendered useless and often the fish either tears itself to pieces or breaks the shaft. For this reason, detachable spearheads are universally recommended for use when hunting pelagic game fish in open water and for bottom fish over 30 pounds. Even experts who can usually stone a 50-pound fish with a multitined head will be the first to admit that for the average diver, a detachable head should be used on everything over 30 pounds. Many of these are simply swinging-barbed, fixed heads, designed to detach after a fish is hit. With these, the shaft will pull free and let the fish fight a cable instead of the harpoon. They are available with the same assortment of cutting tips and rock-point tips as fixed heads, and work fine on all except the largest of fish. For the real monsters of 100 pounds or more, a straight slip-tip with no threads, joints, rivets or other weak points is your best bet. The only disadvantage of a slip-tip is that in order to detach and hold, it must penetrate deeper than a swinging-barbed head, and they are usually more difficult to remove from a fish. But when you are dealing with game weighing 100 pounds or more, your shaft must penetrate almost completely through the fish anyhow and the extra strength and holding power of a slip-tip is of prime importance. Also, with game of this size, quick removal of the spearhead is not a major consideration. In fact, most experts recommend a slip-tip for hunting almost any kind of big game underwater, including fast-moving powerful fish such as yellowtail and amberjack.

Powerheads will convert even a small gun into an extremely powerful and dangerous weapon. They contain a trigger mechanism designed to fire a .22-caliber or .38-caliber cartridge upon impact. The slightest bump will set them off, and the explosion fires a spearhead completely through even the largest fish. All that is necessary is to hit the fish, because the full force of the powerhead is at the point of impact. They are used when hunting extremely large fish such as sharks, grouper, jewfish, etc., which the average gun will not penetrate completely. Some divers believe that the shock of the explosion helps slow a big fish and makes it easier to land. Others discount this theory and insist that the shock of powerheads is due entirely to the speed and penetrating power of the spearhead. No matter which is correct, they are extremely effective when properly designed and rigged, but they can create havoc in the hands of an inexperienced or careless diver.

A gun equipped with a powerhead must be rigged with two lines. The spearhead is usually a straight piece of steel rod inserted into the barrel of the powerhead. It has no barbs or flanges to make it toggle, so if the cartridge doesn't fire, the head pulls out and the fish is not landed. The head travels with the speed of a bullet and sometimes breaks the line tied to it. Most divers prefer nylon to stainless steel cable for powerheads because the flexibility and stretch of nylon will absorb the sudden acceleration, and is less apt to break. The law classes powerheads as firearms with shipping and stor-

Explosive powerheads, armed with a shotgun shell or .357 magnum, fire on impact and blow a large hole in the object they hit. (*Photo by Paul Tzimoulis*)

age under the same restrictions as any other gun. They are extremely dangerous around other divers because when the safety is removed, an accidental bump will fire the powerhead. One model has a safety that is released only by the movement of the spear shaft after the trigger is pulled. In my opinion, this is the only type that is safe to use when other divers are in the water with you.

Other types of powerheads are armed with a shotgun shell or .357-magnum cartridge and do not fire a barb or line into the fish. Their purpose is to kill instantly by blowing a huge hole in the animal they hit. Most of the manufacturers of these weapons, and many divers, claim that the shock of the explosion and the damage caused by the volume of gas expanding into the animal, will kill a shark even if it is not hit in a vital spot. This claim is subject to serious question, and relying too heavily on instant-killing power could get you into trouble. Jim Leonard, a spearfishing champion living in Chicago, reports that he has blasted several sharks with a .357-magnum head and watched the shark swim away at full speed. Other divers swear by these weapons as an excellent defense against sharks, and carry an explosive head on the end of a short pole with them all the time they are in the water. Personally, I prefer to take my chances with the sharks rather than swim with a diver carrying one of these powerheads. I have seen too many nervous, careless, and trigger-happy divers, and had so many safety devices fail to operate, that I'm prejudiced against explosive devices in the hands of most diving companions. I also question the effectiveness of explosive heads as protection against an actual shark attack. They are fine for offensive action, when the diver has time to maneuver into position and place his shot. Even the largest shark is instantly killed when a hole is blown through its head or spine by a shotgun shell. But against a fast-moving shark that is actually attacking, the diver would probably not have time to grab the powerhead and release the safety. If he did, I doubt he could hit a vital spot during the weaving, lightning-fast attack of an incoming shark. However, sharks are completely unpredictable, and an explosive head is a substantial deterrent to those that become too curious.

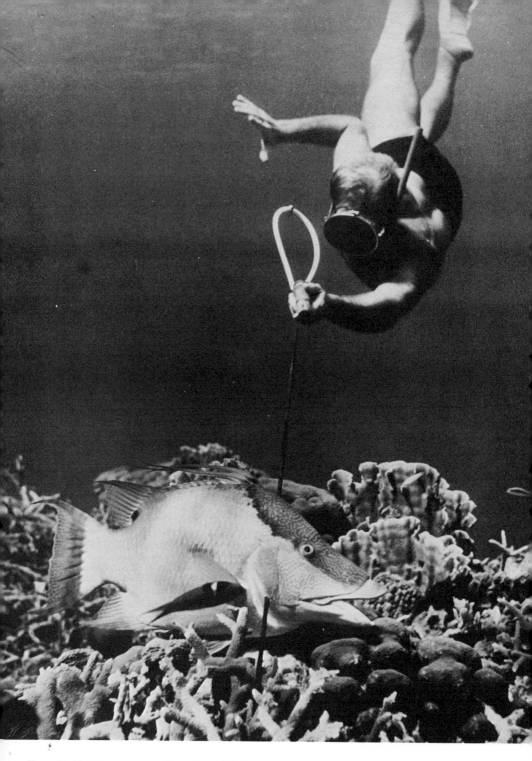

Tom Hubbell scores a perfect shot with his Hawaiian sling off Grand Cayman island, West Indies. (*Photo by Paul Tzimoulis*)

8 *Small Fish for Small Weapons*

THE SPEARFISHERMAN'S adages of "dirty water, short gun; clear water, long gun" and "big fish, big gun; small fish, small gun" are so obvious that repeating them should be unnecessary. But each year a new army of divers equip themselves with the biggest gun they can find, with reel, detachable head and all the extras, and head for the Caribbean or the Pacific to bag a sea monster. These divers fully expect to find the reefs swarming with giant grouper, snappers, jacks and jewfish just begging to be shot. Usually, after half an hour or so of fruitless searching, they give up and start banging away at angelfish, squirrelfish and anything else that swims. This is akin to shooting at rabbits with a 30:06, and is equally ridiculous. At the other extreme, and just as bad, is the diver who carries a small, single-rubber gun with a light line and thinks he is ready for anything. If a 40-pound amberjack or a 60-pound grouper happens to swim into range he doesn't hesitate to shoot. Usually the harpoon will bounce harmlessly off or pull out, but if he is lucky enough to get close and impale the fish, the result is a broken line and a lost harpoon for the diver and a wounded fish that will probably be found floating belly up a few days later.

Another fallacy is one which sometimes traps experienced divers. This is the "all-purpose" gun which the diver tries to use for hunting small fish and large fish at the same time. Hunting fish in this manner is similar to a big-game hunter who insists upon looking for rabbits and squirrels while he really hopes to see a moose or a bear. He doesn't get many rabbits or squirrels, and practically never sees a moose or a bear. I went through the all-purpose-gun stage during my early days of skin diving and it lasted more than a year before an experience with a big fish taught me the fallacy of this approach.

My all-purpose gun was four and one half feet long, equipped with three powerful rubbers, a swinging barb, detachable head and breakaway rigging. It was so awkward and unwieldy that I either missed or passed up most shots at small, fast-moving targets in murky water, and its power was so great that using it for close shots around rocks and caves often banged up the spearhead and bent the shaft. After several frustrating months without seeing a big fish, I became tired of coming in empty handed and reduced the gun's power by hunting with only one of its three rubbers cocked. The two extra rubbers hanging limp at the muzzle were confusing and sometimes got wound up in the harpoon line. The long breakaway line occasionally pulled out and created a tangled mess among the rocks and kelp on the bottom. But I managed to spear a few rockfish, and stubbornly insisted that my all-purpose gun was worth the inconvenience and trouble because of the sea monster I expected to bump into almost any day. A year later, off Anacapa Island, California, my big fish finally came along.

The boat was anchored in a heavy kelp bed, near a shore which plunged sharply down into water about 50 feet deep. I dropped over the side, cocked one of the three rubbers and dived for the bottom. A milky haze clouded the water, limiting visibility and giving the long, leafy strands of kelp an eerie, ghostlike appearance. Swimming through it was like drifting through a forest in a dense fog. No surge or current marred the stillness of the water and the strands of kelp were so quiet that the slightest movement created a major disturbance.

Suddenly, in the dimness at the edge of my range of vision, a patch of kelp began to sway violently back and forth as if caught in a giant whirlwind. I grabbed a rock and braced myself, expecting at any moment to feel the surge of a giant wave, or the strength of some freak underwater current. But the water around me remained calm and I watched the oncoming whirlwind with fascination and wonder. It approached the edge of a clearing about twenty feet away, then one of the largest jewfish I have ever seen broke into the open and began moving slowly toward me. I struggled frantically to cock the extra rubbers of the spear gun as the behemoth cruised into range. Every detail of its huge, gray-black body stood out sharply. The fish was easily seven feet long and so thick that, with its stomach rubbing the bottom, its back was almost as high as a man's head. Its small piglike eyes, large down-turned mouth and undershot jowl gave it an expression of angry surprise. The fish was in no hurry, passing slowly a few feet in front of me, but each movement of its tremendous tail bent the kelp like miniature tidal waves. I was all fingers and thumbs in my hurry to cock the extra rubbers on my gun and the bands tantalizingly hung up in the line or slipped out of my hands. I finished loading just in time to watch the fish disappear in the kelp and see the whirlwind start moving away. Even though the fish was cruising very slowly, my best swimming effort failed to catch it and I never saw the monster again.

The experience taught me several lessons which have proved invaluable. In examining my gun later, I discovered that rockfishing had chafed the line and, had I shot that big fish, it would surely have broken. My accidental encounter with a really big fish had caught me by surprise and not only was my equipment inadequate, I was mentally and psychologically unprepared. I finally realized that an all-purpose spear gun makes about as much sense as an all-purpose rifle, and I decided that a diver has to make up his mind whether he is going after "rabbits" or "bears" before he goes into the water. Only when you know the kind of fish you are hunting can you study their habits and learn where and when to find them. If you just look for fish, you are depending upon luck. When you start looking for a particular species, you become an underwater hunter. Every fish has its own seasons and migratory patterns, and each has its own preference as to terrain, hid-

Australian diver, Barry O'Brien, nails a 30-pound parrot fish with his wooden gun off Gladstone Barrier Reef. (*Photo by Ben Cropp*)

ing places, depth, temperature and food. Only by learning these can you know the kind you are likely to see and the weapon you will need to take it.

There are very few places in the world where big fish can be taken consistently, and in many areas they are never seen at all. Probably only 10 per cent of the world's skin divers have ever seen a fish larger than twenty-five pounds, and even off Southern California and in the Caribbean, the overwhelming majority of fish hunted weigh less than twenty pounds. Even in an area where big fish may be encountered, your chances of seeing one are very slim until you have learned where they live and how to hunt them. So take a small gun along and you won't be caught in the ridiculous position of using an elephant gun to shoot at butterflies.

Small fish are often more elusive and harder to hit than big fish and hunting them is a challenge that has made underwater spearfishing one of the most exciting and satisfying sports in the world. And small fish can be speared in lakes and rivers across the nation as well as in all the oceans of the world. The weapons used are small, but the skills and techniques are often more exciting than for bigger game. By small gun we don't mean the flimsy, cheap, single-band guns so often displayed in department stores which do not specialize in skin diving. These are toys designed to attract youngsters and novices. About all they will kill are tiny perch and colorful reef fish which a true skin diver never shoots. The angelfish, butterfly fish, filefish and other tiny tropicals which decorate a coral reef in a kaleidoscope of moving color, are considered targets for a camera or a collector's net, not a spear gun. These fish are veritable hams, posing and preening in front of a skin diver as if inviting admiration. Shooting them is certainly not a challenge and you will earn the respect of other divers by leaving them for the photographers.

When selecting your spear gun, go to a dive shop or talk to a diving club and learn the kind of weapon local divers are using. A small gun may be any length, from two feet to four feet, but it must be sturdy and pack enough power to impale the tough scales of moderate-size fish. I prefer two rubbers even on a very short weapon, not only because of the extra power they deliver at close range, but, if one of the rubbers should break, I am not completely out of business. Always, on any spear gun, use a strong nylon line that will take a beating around rocks and coral and still hold a fighting fish. If a spear gun won't pull a heavy line and hit with killing impact at a distance three times the length of its spear shaft, the gun is underpowered.

The best spearfishing is usually over a rocky bottom or coral reef that has lots of holes, caves and crevices in which fish can hide to escape their enemies. The underwater terrain is usually a continuation of the adjacent shoreline, and a rocky ridge, point or jetty that extends out into the sea is a good place to hunt. A flat bottom is not as productive as one that is broken, and the face of a reef that drops off into deep water is usually excellent. The quiet waters of harbors, coves, bays and lagoons do not have as many fish as the turbulent waters of an exposed point or an offshore reef. Many reef fish feed upon marine organisms clinging to the rocks, and depend upon wave action or tidal currents to dislodge their food. Offshore reefs in the clear waters of the Caribbean can be spotted by the light-blue coloration of the water above them, and the size and type of reef can be seen with a face mask from the surface. Offshore reefs in the Pacific can be detected by kelp beds growing from the rocks. Some divers in both the Pacific and the Atlantic use boats equipped with a fathometer to locate reefs and wrecks in deep water, and when a new one is found, they have virgin hunting grounds.

Sometimes an apparently barren section of ocean can prove to be a bonanza for spearfishing once a reef is discovered. Puerto Penasco, in the northern section of the Gulf of California, was such an area. For years divers returning from Penasco reported it to be a wasteland, with a shallow, sandy bottom and loose rocks that provided no hiding places for fish. Their observations were proved wrong by Phil Nourse, a member of the Los Angeles Neptunes. Phil scouted the area thoroughly, lying quietly on the surface for hours and watching the antics of small fish playing over the sand beneath him. One day he noticed the small fish were darting in and out of what appeared to be ridges or bumps in the sand. He investigated and discovered that the ridges were actually the edge of a slab of rock formed of fossilized sand. The sand beneath the slab was undermined, leaving a deep, narrow slot which was swarming with fish. Phil put his gun into the slot, aimed at the largest fish he could see and pulled the trigger. The

Bud Columbia displays a prize-winning carp speared in Possum Kingdom Lake, Texas. (*Photo by Bill Barada*)

shaft wedged in the hole and he had quite a struggle getting it out. When it finally broke free, he was surprised to see two fish impaled on his spear. Each fish weighed about twenty pounds and had been wedged into a slot so small they had turned sideways to get between the rock and the sand. Phil's story converted Puerto Penasco into a popular diving spot, and today other skin divers can be seen snorkeling on the surface watching a school of small fish to see if they will lead them to an invisible reef.

Observing the activities of small fish is an excellent way to locate larger game. Fish are afflicted with diseases and parasites just as are other animals, and certain reefs are "cleaning stations" where tiny cleaner fish act as doctors, picking off parasites and chewing away unhealthy tissue of larger fish. The phenomena is called symbiosis, and the cleaner fish are granted immunity from attack. They even go inside the mouth of larger fish to clean their teeth and throat. Many scientists believe that the world's great fishing banks may be giant cleaning stations to which game fish are attracted in large numbers. Watching the aquabatics of these tiny, colorful cleaners as they advertise for customers is not only an interesting pastime, the cleaners may also be signaling that you have found a good reef for spearfishing.

Schools of bait fish are another sign that often indicate a good fishing-reef area. These are forage for game fish and the quarry you are seeking may be lurking in the rocks below or hanging out of sight in the distance. Following a school of bait and prowling the bottom beneath it can pay off with some interesting and exciting catches.

Many reef fish hide inside the reef all day or "hole up" at the first indication of danger. Hunting these means prowling the bottom and peering into every nook and cranny in the same manner that is used when hunting lobsters. Don't concentrate only on the large holes and caves. The fish prefer to hide in spaces only a little bigger than their body so a larger predator can't get at them. The entrances to many good fish holes are nothing more than an insignificant crack between two rocks. When you put your face close and peer inside, it often opens out into a larger cavern that is swarming with all sizes and kinds of fish. Spotting a good fish hole is often only a matter of persistent bottom scrounging, but a few telltale signs sometimes can be a tip-off. Any jumble of rocks or section of reef that has a lot of small fish dart-

Sometimes an apparently barren section of ocean can prove to be a bonanza for spearfishing once a reef or wreck is discovered. Here a school of chub swim past a piece of wreckage. (*Photo by Paul Tzimoulis*)

ing around it should be carefully checked. Fish have runways on a reef similar to animals in a forest, and the seaweed grass and marine organisms are often worn away around the entrance of a well-used hole. Sometimes the rocks look almost as if they have been polished by the hundreds of thousands of fish that have passed over them.

Good marksmanship is just as important in spearfishing as it is in game hunting, and aiming in the general direction of a fish is just as big a mistake as it is with land animals. The novice has a tendency to be overanxious and take long shots while the fish is too far away or out of position. His spear shaft often bounces off, doesn't penetrate deeply enough to hold or hits in a soft portion of the fish's body and is

torn out by its struggles. A skilled spearfisherman stalks his fish until
he is close enough to place the harpoon in a vital spot, and he always
tries for a kill shot that will stone the fish immediately. Never aim for
the tail or the soft underbelly in the lower half of the body, as the harpoon will almost invariably tear out. It is usually not a good idea to
shoot at a fish while it is looking at you head on. It not only offers a
poor target, you are shooting at the most streamlined position of the
fish and your spear will probably bounce off its bony head or glance
off the scales without penetrating. Small fish can be shot in the head
if you are close enough to split the skull and penetrate almost solid
bone. The gills also are a hard bony structure that will deflect a spear
if hit at an angle or shot from too far away. On a broadside shot, the
best place to aim is a point just behind the gills and in line with or just
above the eyes. This will sever the spine and stone the fish. If you miss
the spine, the spear is imbedded in the toughest and boniest part of
the fish and the barbs are likely to hold. Coming down on a fish from
above, aim for the center of its back just behind the head and again
you have a good chance of getting a kill shot by severing the spine.
Many divers, when shooting at a good-sized fish that is broadside but
angled slightly toward them, have been surprised to see a heavy shaft
bounce harmlessly off without penetrating the fish. The reason is that
some fish have thick scales that are as hard as glass, and they act like
armor plate to deflect the spear. Whenever possible, it is best to shoot
when the fish is angled away from you, so the spear point can slide
between the scales and penetrate the body. This is especially true of
extremely large fish such as giant grouper and jewfish, where even a
shaft from a powerful spear gun can be deflected or stopped by the
heavy scales.

Accurate shooting with a spear gun is more like handling a pistol
than a rifle, and an expert handles his weapon with the skill of an old
Western gunfighter. In crystal clear water, when shooting at sitting or
slow-moving targets, you may be able to take the time to sight and aim
your spear gun like a rifle. But at moving targets, you are in a fluid
medium with everything in motion, similar to a gunfighter on horse-
back, and you must be able to fire accurately by instinct as if your gun
were an extension of your arm. In dirty water, snap shooting is even
more necessary because you often have only a fraction of a second be-

The great barracuda of tropical waters are fair game for skin divers. To make a "kill shot," aim for a spot just behind the gills, in line with its eyes. This photo is an actual barracuda kill, in 85 feet of water off Curaçao, Netherlands Antilles. (*Photo by Paul Tzimoulis*)

fore the fish is out of sight. A hunter who must always approach his target head on in order to line up for a shot will scare a lot of fish away and pass up easy shots. One of the tricks in stalking fish is to pretend not to look directly at it. Constantly staring at a fish can make it so spooky that it never comes into range. Try watching it from the corner of your eye and swim at an angle slightly away from its direction, or lie quietly and wait for the fish to come in. A fish may approach within range from either side, the rear, above, or below; and you must be able to shoot without turning your body in its direction. In holes and caves or in very dirty water, you will often have to fire with the handle of the gun drawn back even with your hip because you can't see the spear tip with the gun extended. At other times, the fish is so close your shaft will project beyond it.

Every spear gun and every harpoon handles and fires a little differently and the wise spearfisherman practices with his gun until he can aim and shoot as instinctively as pointing his finger. Practice must be done underwater. Firing a spear gun in the air is useless, dangerous and will ruin most underwater weapons. A good method is to trace a circle in the sand at a comfortable depth and practice shooting at it from every conceivable angle. Remove the spearhead and line to save the time and inconvenience of rerigging after every shot. Their absence won't affect the accuracy of your gun. Firing at kelp leaves, seaweed and objects in the water is good practice, but doesn't let you see exactly where your shot is hitting, as will a harpoon imbedded in the sand. When you can hit the center of the circle four out of five times while snap shooting from every angle, you are approaching the ability of a spearfishing champion.

If you live inland where sandy beaches and clear water are not available, try to find an owner of a swimming pool who will let you take a spear gun into the water. Anchor a target, such as a foam plastic or cork float, a few feet off the bottom and practice shooting at it. Be sure the target is large enough to insure that you don't miss it completely and damage the pool. A short line attached to the harpoon will prevent its escape in case of a ricochet or missed shot.

Hitting a fish is sometimes only the beginning of a battle. Unless a fish is stoned there is always a chance that it will manage to tear itself off the shaft, and even one that appears to be killed will often come to life and put up a terrific struggle. Many a diver, heading happily to the surface with a prize fish dangling from his spear, has been dismayed to find his harpoon empty when he reached the boat. After a fish is hit, the surest way to insure your catch is to swim down the harpoon line and get it in your hands. If the harpoon has penetrated completely through the fish, you can grab the shaft with one hand on each side to quiet its struggles and prevent escape. If the barbs are imbedded inside the fish, grabbing it by the head with a finger in each eye will paralyze the fish and give you a good grip that is unlikely to slip off. Sometimes you can get your fingers in its gills, but be careful of tropical fish such as the Gulf grouper. These fish have long gill rakers as sharp as needles that can close down on your hand and

The holes, crevices and grottoes of a reef are productive hunting areas. Allen Caperton nails a good one in a reef off Cozumel Island, Mexico. (*Photo by Mick Church*)

cause a painful wound. I made this mistake on a 25-pounder off Tiburon Island in Baja California and it almost cost me my hand.

I was free diving and, when I hit the fish, it holed up in the rocks with its body turned sideways so the harpoon couldn't pull it out. I put my hand into its gills, intending to turn the fish, and felt the gill rakers clamp down. It was like having my hand caught by a bunch of oversize needles all pointing at an angle toward the inside of the fish. Pulling to free my hand only drove the rakers deeper into my flesh. I couldn't turn the fish and my situation became desperate when I began gulping for air. Finally I had no choice but to brace my shoulders against the rock, grit my teeth and give a mighty tug. My hand came free, but a heavy leather glove and part of the flesh on each finger stayed inside the fish. I reached surface with my hand bleeding profusely from a dozen lacerations that penetrated to the bone. After some quick first aid I dived down to get the fish, but this time I kept my hands out of its gills.

Women's spearfishing champion, Mary Edith Lillis, literally climbs a tree underwater to spear carp in Table Rock Lake, Missouri. Mel prefers murky water for best carp hunting. (*Photo by Bill Barada*)

When hunting small fish in holes, it is best to use a short line and pull the fish out while it is still stunned from the impact. If you are using scuba and the fish hangs up, you can take your time about digging it out. When free diving and a fish hangs up, if your line is too short to reach the surface, let the gun go and try again with a fresh lungful of air. If the line is long enough to reach to a float on the surface, loop the line through a rope or strap on the float and pull downward. This will put a constant strain on the fish until it eventually becomes tired and gives up.

In clear water you can sometimes spot your game from the surface or drift 10 or 15 feet above the bottom looking for targets. When a fish is out of range, you can play games of hide-and-seek, watching its reactions, until you get close enough for a shot. In dirty water, you must hunt blind, because you never see a fish until it is already in range. The fish have the advantage because they detect your presence long before you can see them, and your only hope is to play upon their curiosity or find them hiding in holes.

Most states permit fresh-water spearfishing for rough fish such as carp, buffalo and suckers, but the majority of the lakes have water so dirty you can't see your hand in front of your face mask. The best diving is usually in man-made lakes which are too new to have become thoroughly polluted, but even in these, a day when you can see 15 feet is considered excellent. The creation of a man-made lake floods a river bed, inundating trees and brush along the bank. This underwater forest is still standing on the bottom and provides interesting diving as well as excellent hiding places for the fish. The prime target of fresh-water spearfishermen is carp, a golden-brown fish which feeds on algae and moss. Specimens have been taken weighing well over 40 pounds, but the majority weigh between 5 and 15 pounds. They are a free-swimming fish which like to hide around sunken logs, brush and rock piles and the dirtier the water, the better a carp likes it. They are very spooky, shying away at the slightest noise or movement, and a careless diver is lucky if he ever sees one. The technique for hunting carp in inland lakes is one example of playing upon a fish's curiosity. I watched champions Mary Edith (Mel) Lillis and June Poplar of the Midwest Council of Diving Clubs during competition at Table Rock

Lake, Missouri, and their performances were revelations in patience and perseverance.

Table Rock Lake was formed by a dam across the White River in the Ozark Mountains and has the usual underwater forest. On the day of the contest, vision was so limited that another diver ten feet away in the water appeared as fuzzy and indistinct as a silhouette in a dense fog. To my surprise the lady divers, Mel and June, complained that the water was too clear for good fishing. But, after I watched their technique, the complaint was understandable. They literally climbed a tree underwater and waited for a carp to swim within range. The contest lasted four hours and most of this time the girls spent wrapped around the trunk of a tree or sitting motionless on a branch, breathing quietly from their scuba and waiting for a curious carp to be attracted by their bubbles. When the water was clear the fish were extra cautious and stayed out of the diver's range of vision.

Dick Neuman, of the Lakeshore Club in Texas, claims that carp will be found within a few feet of the same depth on a given day. Once you see your first carp, you should stay at that depth because the fish will be concentrated at the same level. He also says that dragging a speared carp on a line or fish stringer will attract others which follow the dead fish. Dick advises that you string the fish through its eyes so it will be free moving and look natural in the water.

John Hoynacki, who runs a dive shop at Indian Point on Table Rock Lake has a unique method of attracting carp into range. I witnessed his technique while diving with John in an extremely dirty section of the lake. The end of a two-foot spear gun I was carrying disappeared from sight if I held it at arms length. I hunted quietly for an hour without seeing a single fish. Finally, near a clump of brush growing out of the water, I began to hear a peculiar burbling noise, foreign to any of the natural sounds around the lake. The noise continued intermittently for several minutes, then two large carp swam by beneath me headed in the direction of the sound. Next, I heard the twang of a spear gun and John came up from behind the bushes with a carp impaled on the end of his spear. When asked about the sound, John admitted that he used this technique consistently and found it very effective. The noise was John "talking" into his snorkel.

Another fresh-water fish which gives divers great sport is the alli-

John Hoynacki displays a 20-pound carp speared in Table Rock Lake, Missouri. John calls carp by "talking" into his snorkel. (*Photo by Bill Barada*)

gator gar found in the lakes and swamps of Louisiana and Texas. Most gar are in the small-fish class, weighing between 10 and 20 pounds, but some grow to a tremendous size. Joe Coffield of Shreveport, Louisiana holds the skin-diving record for a gar speared in Caddo Lake, Louisiana that measured seven feet, four inches and weighed 140 pounds. The Texas Park and Wildlife Commission records show gar taken from Caddo Lake that weighed 500 pounds. The gar is a unique, ugly fish that looks like a cross between an alligator and a lizard. Its hide and scales are so hard that sparks fly when the fish is hit with an ax and spearing them demands a razor-sharp spear point and use of the right technique. They are only hunted in the middle of winter, when the gar lie dormant on the bottom and the water in Caddo "clears up" to give visibility of 18 inches. Dick Wil-gus of Longview, Texas says that gar are usually found lying camou-flaged in sunken logs and not in moss. The larger ones are in deeper water, below 30 feet, and only small ones stay as shallow as eight to ten feet. He recommends that you follow a zigzag pattern, swimming in and out of the murky layer near the bottom. Dick advises never to shoot at a gar that is facing toward you or broadside, as your spear will only bounce off the heavy scales. Use a short gun with powerful rubbers and a short length of line so you can prevent the fish from becoming tangled in the brush and weeds.

Most of the tactics used in fresh water can be used for dirty-water hunting in the ocean. When using scuba, the technique used by Mel Lillis and June Poplar is excellent. Dan Nelson, of New Orleans, tells of taking sheepshead in water with one-foot visibility by this method. The Gulf sheepshead should not be confused with the Pacific fish of the same name. The Gulf fish is distinguished by black-and-white ver-tical stripes and a big one weighs 15 pounds. A male Pacific sheeps-head reaches weights of over 30 pounds and is reddish-brown in color, with a large white patch on its jaw. Dan's system is to make him-self comfortable on the bottom with his back against a rock or the piling of a pier, with his gun between his legs and pointing upward. Dan says that, if you don't move, and breathe so quietly that you sip your air as if sucking it through a straw, eventually a curious sheepshead will swim in front of your mask. Sometimes you must sit still for as long as ten or fifteen minutes, and usually all you will see are the white stripes of the fish. But, if you want to spear a sheepshead in the dirty waters of the Gulf of Mexico, Dan says that's the way to do it.

When free diving in dirty water, the tactics are very similar, except that a diver can keep moving because there are no bubbles to warn the fish of his approach. Frank Xedus, a champion spearfisherman in Wilmington, Delaware says that the fish most sought by skin divers along the East Coast is the blackfish (tautog) which grows as long as three feet, with weights of over 20 pounds. They are a free-swimming fish found from Maine to the Carolinas. Some divers hunt them with scuba in deep water around offshore wrecks, but Frank prefers free diving around rock piles and jetties near shore. He says, "Most of the time we have very poor visibility. If we have two or three feet, we can get some fish; if we can see six to eight feet, we can get all the fish we want, and sometimes we can get a fish or two when we can see only six inches to one foot. When spearfishing, you do everything slow, and in poor visibility you do it even slower. Most of our shooting is done from the hip in order to keep the point of the spear as far back as possible so the fish won't be scared off before we see it. I use a small gun, but with heavier and shorter slings to give it more power. For the last four years I have been using a five-prong spearhead because it gives more margin for error when hip shooting."

In dirty water many fish hiding among the shadows of a cave cannot be seen without the aid of a light. Some divers carry a flashlight mounted on their gun, but most prefer to hold the light in their free hand in order to cover more of the inside of the hole. A strap or band should be used to attach the handle of the light to your wrist, so both hands are free to string the fish and reload your gun. A pressure-proof flashlight can be used underwater, but the more powerful, dry-cell-type diving lights will give better results. A weak light can produce a lot of frustration if you suspect that a big fish is hiding just beyond the beam. Even in the Caribbean, an underwater light will produce extra dividends when cave fishing. But, for pelagic, free-swimming fish in open water, different techniques and equipment must be used.

A flock of diving sea birds often guide you to the location of game fish. Note the various flight attitudes of these pelicans diving off Acapulco, Mexico. (*Photo by Mick Church*)

9 Open Water Game Fish—
Choice of the Experts

THE 16-FOOT outboard, *Chapulin,* bounced and leaped over the whitecaps as playfully as the grasshopper for which it was named. We were headed for Todos Santos Island, five miles out in the Pacific off Ensenada, Mexico, and Homer Lockwood of the Inglewood Sharks Diving Club handled the boat with the dexterity of a cowboy on a galloping horse. As the island loomed closer we scanned the surface of the sea for signs of activity that would indicate the location of our quarry. A flurry of motion in the distance caught my eye. A flock of sea gulls, pelicans and other birds were swirling and diving, the splash of their bodies hitting the water was mixed with the occasional boil of a large fish striking from below the surface. Homer headed the boat in their direction, a smile of delighted anticipation lighting his face like a hunter who has sighted a herd of deer. "Yellowtail," he said happily. "It looks like a big school."

We anchored the boat 500 yards off the island and paid out 200 feet of rope before the anchor hit the bottom. Birds were diving all around us, picking sardines out of the school that swarmed near the surface. Occasionally the boil and splash of a large fish sent the bait scurrying across the water in a panicky flight that sounded like the rustle of leaves in an autumn wind. We hurried into our gear, grabbed our guns and slipped over the side. This was free diving. The only scuba on board was strictly for emergency or trouble. Yellowtail can be taken with scuba, but the mobility of free diving increased our chances of getting within range of these speed merchants.

Floating on the surface, I looked down at a sight that makes a spearfisherman's blood tingle with excitement. We were in open water. No kelp, rocks or bottom could be seen, only the clear blue water of the Pacific. Around me, into the depths as far as I could see, schools of tiny sardines dotted the water, weaving and turning in close-packed flight, their ranks thinned by constant attack from predators above and below. A dozen yellowtail were in view; silvery bellies' flashing, they swam in wolf-pack formation, zigzagging through the water like a squadron of fighters on a mission. I hyperventilated with a dozen forced inhalations and exhalations, then slipped beneath the surface and swam slowly downward. Only my flippers moved, the rest of my body was held motionless, and I made no attempt to direct myself toward the fish. At 30 feet I quit swimming and hung dead in the water, watching the yellowtail out of the corner of my eye. The fish started a wide circle, their curiosity stimulated. I continued to hang motionless but moved my free hand to the gun and began strumming the rubbers with my fingers. The sound vibrated through the water and I saw a yellowtail break out of the pack and head in my direction. I moved the gun into position, waited until the fish was about eight feet away and turning broadside, then pulled the trigger. The shaft struck just behind the gills. I felt a tug as the fish streaked off. The breakaway line began to pay out. I grabbed the line, exerted a gentle tension like the drag on a fishing reel and headed for the surface. The line sang through my fingers, and I could feel the heat through my leather gloves. The tension tired the fish and I still had the line left when my snorkel broke into the air. Lying on the surface, I played the fish cautiously until it was completely spent, then started pulling it in. The school of yellowtail followed the dead fish and, had I held a second gun, I could have shot another fish.

My yellowtail weighed 25 pounds and it was the only one I landed that day. I cruised for hours trying every trick I knew, but they stayed out of range, never coming close enough for another shot. Homer Lockwood did better. Once I watched him dive on an interception course as a school approached. He drove straight ahead with his spear gun and body as rigid and streamlined as an arrow. His timing was perfect and as the fish veered away to avoid collision, he picked off the leader with a beautiful shot through the head.

Homer landed three yellowtail that day, but only two had spear holes in them. One fish he actually took away from a sea lion that was having trouble getting its teeth into the slippery, 20-pound yellowtail. Homer watched the struggle from the surface for a while. The fish was stunned and unable to swim, probably the sea lion had stolen it from some fisherman's line. Each time the sea lion tried to bite the fish it squirted out of its mouth, toward the surface and toward Homer. When the fish squirted close, Homer dived, grabbed its tail and took it away from the sea lion. The angry, frustrated sea lion went into a series of dazzling aquabatics, circling, diving, then rushing at Homer with its teeth bared. Several times they engaged in a tug of war, the sea lion pulling on the fish's head and Homer hanging onto the tail. Once on the surface, Homer used the fish as a club and banged the sea lion over the head. That discouraged it. I guess the sea lion was convinced that a diver this stubborn would never give up the fish. It swam away and we never saw it again.

Pelagic (open water) fish such as yellowtail, tuna, white sea bass, wahoo, dolphin, pompano and jacks are seldom seen by the average skin diver. These are deep-ocean fish found in open water, usually near the surface, and they depend upon speed, stamina and agility to escape their enemies rather than hiding in holes and caves of a reef. Occasionally one will be taken by a diver prowling the bottom of near-shore reefs, but this is almost as rare as a hunter getting a shot at an antelope while he is hunting for deer. In most cases, hunting pelagic fish is a special form of spearfishing that requires the knowledge, skill and patience of a hunter stalking Rocky Mountain sheep. These are the ones on which long-range guns, razor-sharp detachable heads, breakaway rigging or reels, floats and, in some cases, powerheads are used extensively. All of these fish have terrific speed and power on

Even sailfish can be taken by an expert spearfisherman who is willing to cross swords with them. (*Photo by Bill Barada*)

their initial rush and some, such as the amberjack, are so strong they can tow a 200-pound diver through the water for long distances. Some divers delight in shooting these fish with a short line or stainless steel cable and "riding it out" underwater. This is fine if you are using scuba and hunting in an area with a great expanse of shallow bottom where the fish can't drag you into deep water. But if the bottom is 200 feet or deeper, and the fish heads straight down, even a scuba diver must let go of his gun or he may never see the surface again. An example of this occurred at Cabo San Lucas on the tip of Baja California where amberjack have collected enough spear guns to stock a dive shop.

The harbor at Cabo San Lucas is unique in that its shallow, sandy bottom is bounded by precipitous underwater canyons which plunge thousands of feet into the abyss. One of these canyons terminates near the end of a pier used by the local fish cannery. Effluent from the cannery attracts millions of small fish, and a diver standing on the pier can look down at a school of bait so thick the water is black with their bodies. Large migratory fish, such as yellowtail, barracuda, pompano and jacks move up through the canyon to attack the school. At times large schools of yellowtail hit the bait in such numbers that the surface of the water is churned into a froth from their attack. On almost any day a diver working the school will find at least a few stray amberjack feeding on the bait and he might see anything from giant sea bass, grouper and snapper to rare deep-water dolphin and blue-fin tuna. I visited Cabo San Lucas with my 19-year-old son, Dick, who was eager to spear his first big fish. His experience with an amberjack taught him why the Mexicans have named this species "pez fuerte" or strong fish.

Our guide was Don Scott, a native of San Diego who had migrated to Mexico and opened a skin diver's resort. Dick had been using a powerful, three-rubber spear gun equipped with 200 feet of nylon line attached to a reel. This worked well on grouper and snapper in the shallow Gulf, but at Cabo San Lucas, Don advised Dick to use his gun. It was a beautiful weapon with a wooden stock almost six feet long, carved out of polished mahogany. But the unique feature was the method of rigging. Don's harpoon line was 50 feet of ¼-inch nylon rope attached directly from the shaft to an inner tube floating on the surface. Loops of line were coiled to pay out with the shaft. The rest trailed behind in the water to tow the inner tube. When he fired, the gun was free in his hands and only the shaft, line and inner tube stayed with the fish. The inner tube may have saved my son's life.

We used scuba to explore the school of bait. Dick carried the spear gun and I followed with a camera. Diving through the school was like diving through a tunnel. A solid wall of bait opened before us as we descended, and immediately enclosed us in a living, moving wall of sea life. Sunlight was partially obscured and we swam in a shadowy world where vision was indistinct. The constant movement of the dense cloud of fish gave us an eerie sensation, as if floating in the vortex of a whirlpool. One moment we were surrounded by thousands of angelfish and a few seconds later we were in the midst of a school of triggerfish. We never knew what form of sea life was hunting its dinner in the same school and swimming unseen a few feet away.

The fish wall opened and disclosed an amberjack directly in line with Dick's gun. His shaft hit the fish just behind the gills and the amberjack laid over as if stoned. Dick raced down the line to get his fingers in its eyes before the fish came to life. He touched the fish, I saw a flurry of motion, and both Dick and the amberjack disappeared. I surfaced and saw the inner tube being pulled across the water with such power that it was standing on end. There was no sign of Dick, and I had several anxious minutes before his head finally bobbed to the surface.

Dick told me later that the instant he touched the fish his mask was knocked off and he felt himself being dragged through the water at terrific speed by a loop of line wrapped around his wrist. The amberjack headed straight for the bottom of the canyon and, without the inner tube, Dick might have been towed hundreds of feet into the depths. Dick said, "I opened my eyes and saw my mask hanging to the line only a few inches from my nose. So I put it back on, cleared it, worked my wrist free and swam to the surface." The amberjack that did all that only weighed 35 pounds.

These fish reach weights well over 100 pounds, and Don Scott says that California divers are constantly losing spear guns because they insist upon hunting Cabo San Lucas amberjack with a reel instead of a surface float.

Another expert who prefers not to use a reel when hunting game fish is Ron Merker, who is co-owner with Omar Wood of the Aquatic Center Dive Shop in Newport Beach, California. Ron and Omar are skilled at all kinds of underwater hunting, but Ron's specialty is white sea bass, probably the most wary and most difficult of all game fish to spear. Few west coast spearfishermen have ever seen a white sea bass. Hundreds have hunted them persistently and never landed one, and a diver who brings in two or three in a single season is considered an expert. Ron Merker speared and landed seven white sea bass in one day.

The white sea bass is not really a bass, but a drum, and it ranges the Pacific coast from Alaska to Baja California. However, they are seldom taken by divers north of Point Conception because the water

A fighting fish is paralyzed by gripping its eye sockets. Dick Barada lands a 30-pound red snapper off Cabo San Lucas, Mexico. (*Photo by Bill Barada*)

The Pacific white sea bass is probably the most difficult of all fish to spear, and are so wary that the majority of divers never see one. Ron Merker, of Aquatic Center Dive Shop, Newport Beach, California, displays 3 taken in one day off Catalina Island, California. (*Photo courtesy of U. S. Diver's Co.*)

is usually too dirty. They are a beautiful fish with silvery-white bodies that grow to lengths of six feet and weights of more than 80 pounds. They spawn in spring and summer around kelp beds. The white sea bass season starts in April and runs through October, with the best hunting during June and July. They may be hunted all year, but only a few, wise old mossbacks hang around during the winter and they are usually very deep, very spooky and extremely difficult to approach.

A unique characteristic of the whites is their apparent lack of curiosity regarding a skin diver. Unlike most other fish, they cannot be enticed into changing their direction and never swim close to look you over. Divers can attract cobia, yellowtail, jacks and pompano by wiggling their fingers, flashing their diving watch, tapping on their spear gun and hanging dead in the water. But Ron Merker says, "Whites continue on their normal way and, if you do something to distract them, you will see their eyeballs roll, then 'boom,' they are gone!" Adding to the prestige of whites is the fact that they are strictly a free-diver's fish. Thousand of divers have hunted whites with scuba and, although they see them occasionally, I don't know of a single case where one has been landed by a diver wearing a tank.

The white sea bass are usually found around the outer edges of the kelp beds toward the open ocean and on out, perhaps 75 or 100 yards into blue water. Divers watch for schools of speckled perch, which they call white sea bass bait, and they work these schools hoping a white sea bass will come along. However, Ron Merker says that whites may be taken in kelp from four feet deep on out to blue water, perhaps 20 yards beyond the kelp. Farther out they are so deep you can't see them, or if you do, you can't get to them. Each diver has his own pet spots where he looks for fish and Ron says, "Don't listen to the guys who are willing to tell you where these places are. Either they don't know, won't say or they lie to you because no spearfisherman wants his pet spots swarming with divers."

The size and thickness of a kelp bed is no indication that it is inhabited by whites. Some large, extensive kelp beds have been hunted for years and have never produced a white sea bass. Other thin beds with only a few strands showing on the surface are regular hangouts for these fish and divers can expect to see them almost every time they visit the area. Ron Merker says he has one choice spot at Catalina Island with only a single, lonely stalk of kelp growing. But every time he dives there, he sees at least one white.

The best hunting grounds for whites are the offshore islands because the water along the mainland is often so dirty that a fish cannot be seen at any distance. In dirty water, and even in the clear water off Catalina, a good way to hunt is to look for "sleepers" hanging motionless in the kelp a few feet beneath the surface. The white sea bass sometimes hides with its head practically on the surface. The technique is to drop down about ten feet and slowly cruise the kelp lanes,

watching for the shapes and outlines of fish hiding in the clumps.
Your surface dives must be as quiet as a seal's, and you must be careful not to disturb the kelp or make any noise while you are breathing
through your snorkel on the surface. A diver who is constantly waving his arms and legs to keep his equilibrium or who splashes the surface with his flippers, will never see a sleeping white. Ron Merker says that even when the fish are swimming, a flipper slap on the
surface will warn the fish and scare them away. If the fish are deep,
they must be approached with a minimum of movement. He says,
"Swim slowly, and keep watching the fish's eyes. Keep watching its
head. Its eyes will give you an indicator just before it goes, and, once
you see this sign, shoot, no matter how close you are. If you are too
far away to see its eyes, you can read the warning signs by the movement of its head. Learning to read these indicator signs accurately
spells the difference between the guys who get whites and those who
don't." Ron also says that the reason so few divers see white sea bass
is that they make too many mistakes and scare them away long before
they ever get near.

Ron's advice to divers who want to hunt white sea bass is, "The
deeper you can work, free diving, the better off you are. Most free
divers can work to depths of 20 feet, some can work to depths of 30
feet and only a few can reach 40 feet. If you can free dive to depths
between 40 and 60 feet, you will be working water that is seldom hit
and your chances of getting fish are a lot greater."

Big Jim Christiansen, a world-champion spearfisherman with fantastic ability, supports Ron's contention about deep diving. Jim takes
white sea bass regularly off Ship Rock at Catalina Island where they
habitually run very deep. The rock forms an underwater precipice
which drops straight down to depths of over 100 feet. Jim's technique
is to start his dive some distance away from the wall, drop down to
around 60 feet, then start slowly moving toward the rocks. This traps
the fish between Jim and the rock, and he has a better chance of cutting them off before they bolt.

The best weapon for white sea bass is the longest range gun you
can handle. They are not a fish that will swim up to you, and if the
closest you can get is 30 feet, you must have a gun that will put a
spearhead in a fish at that distance. Ron doesn't like the term "killing

Astronaut-Aquanaut Scott Carpenter surfaces with a nice Nassau grouper speared on Palancar Reef off Cozumel Island, Mexico. Commander Carpenter was the U. S. Navy's senior aquanaut on Sealab III. (*Photo by Chuck Nicklin*)

range" or "kill shot." He says, "All I try to do is put a head in the fish and tire it out. You can't shoot a fish 30 feet away and pick the spot you intend to hit. I say pick the middle of the fish that offers the biggest target and where you have good solid meat to hold the barbs." Ron prefers a breakaway rather than a reel because the end of the line can be attached to an inflatable float, separate from the gun. If a big fish is hit while working deep and you can't make it back to the surface, a breakaway and inflatable float will let you save your gun. With a line attached to a reel, you must also let the gun go.

You don't take whites or any of the speedy game fish by spending a half hour or an hour in the water and calling it a day's fishing. White sea bass experts are willing to spend six to eight hours in the water and call it a good day if they even see one. This is why mistakes are so costly. If you blow a shot, you have often blown the whole day.

Other pelagic fish may be hunted in much the same way as white sea bass and yellowtail. Most are migratory fish which follow warm water northward along the Pacific and Atlantic coasts in the spring and summer, and some move close inshore to spawn around rocky points and islands. Jacks, cobia and drum can be hunted around sunken wrecks along the Atlantic coast and schools of bluefish, weakfish and even tuna can be spotted in the open ocean by watching for flocks of diving sea birds, or the surface boil of big fish feeding on a school of bait. Some skin divers hunt open water fish in the same manner used by rod-and-reel fishermen. They carry a tank of live bait and troll with feathered jigs or lures until they get a strike. Then, by chumming with handfuls of live bait they can sometimes bring the school to the surface and go after them with spear guns.

In the Caribbean, the deep water along the outer edge of a coral reef is hunted in much the same manner as the kelp beds and rocky reefs of the Pacific. Long-range guns, breakaway rigging, reels and surface floats can be used for these fish in almost all waters. However, there is one unique area where this equipment is useless. That area is the water beneath the oil rigs off the coasts of Louisiana and Texas.

The Gulf of Mexico off Louisiana is a delta of the Mississippi River, with a bottom composed of mud, silt and debris extending for hundreds of miles in all directions. The sea bottom is so shallow that in many places 30 miles offshore, the water is still only 30 feet deep. It is the richest offshore-oil-producing region on earth, and thousands of structures dot the surface all the way from shore to more than 100 miles at sea. Beneath each of these structures is a maze of pilings, cross members and risers that serve as artificial reefs providing protection and a food supply in an otherwise barren ocean. Before oil rigs were planted in the Gulf, the mud bottom would not support clinging marine organisms and the plankton and spawn of small fish drifting into the area sank to the bottom and perished. The basic food chain could not get started and game fish in the Gulf were practically unheard of. Now, the oil rigs offer the most prolific fishing grounds I have ever seen. The pilings, stanchions and rigging beneath each rig are encrusted with coral, gorgonia, sea urchins and a thousand other marine organisms that thrive and multiply on these man-made reefs. Small fish find an abundance of food and they also thrive and multiply under the protection of the rigs. This ready-made food supply attracts

Divers have learned that the great barracuda are just big fish with sharp teeth, which can be hunted the same as any other species. (*Photo by Paul Tzimoulis*)

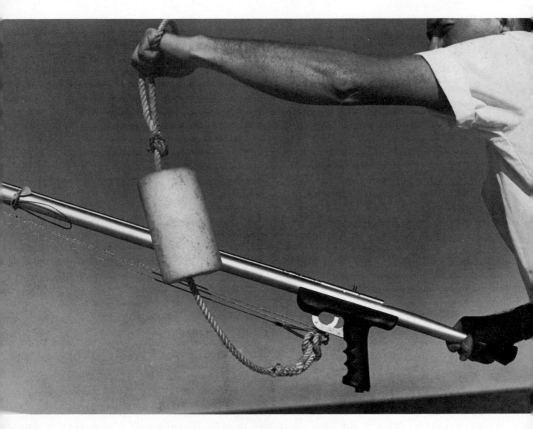

A "riding rig" is used to land large fish beneath the offshore-oil rigs of Louisiana. The diver hangs onto the rope handle and rides until he or the fish becomes too tired to continue. (*Photo by Bill Barada*)

large, migratory game fish which return in greater numbers every year. The concentration of fish around an oil rig is almost unbelievable and although they don't offer the colorful beauty of tropical coral reefs, or the mystery and excitement of Pacific kelp beds, rig divers have the beauty of moving sea life and the greatest hunting in the world.

Spearfishing under the rigs is different from any other area. Most of the diving is from 20 to 60 miles from shore, and storms, bad weather and dirty water limit the season to the summer months. Between May and September, gentle south winds push the dirty, muddy water close to shore and the water is calm enough for a small boat to venture safely 50 miles out into the Gulf. At other times of the year strong winds blow from the north, pushing the muddy Mississippi water as far as 100 miles or more into the Gulf, and the water is so turbulent and unpredictable that even commercial-diving companies seldom try to work. The best months are June, July and August, when the water is usually calm and clear and the big fish are in.

Hunting fish under rigs is like hunting in a man-made forest of steel and concrete which extends all the way to the bottom, sometimes more than 200 feet. A big fish, speared in this jungle, weaves in and out of the structure in a frantic effort to escape. All of the usual methods of rigging are useless. The barnacles and coral cut a nylon line as if it were twine. Breakaway rigging, reels, surface floats and other long-line methods of holding a big fish do not work because the line becomes hopelessly tangled in the maze, and either breaks or the spearhead pulls out. Practically all spearfishing is done with scuba, and rig divers use a short length of stainless steel cable that will stand the abuse of coral and barnacles without breaking. When they hit a fish, they ride it out, close hauled, until either the diver or the fish become too tired to continue. Some divers use a "riding rig" in which the cable is attached to a short loop of rope free of their gun. When they shoot, they hold the rope in one hand and the gun in the other. And when they hit a big fish, they hang on for dear life as the fish tries to dislodge them by dodging and weaving through the structure.

Almost any type of fish may be hunted around the same rig, and a diver can take his choice of free-swimming fish or bottom-dwelling species. However, pelagic fish prefer the clear water usually found around deep rigs 50 to 100 miles from shore, while the giant jewfish are more often found on the bottom of shallow rigs in less than 30 feet of water. The same type of gun, rigging and techniques are used on all kinds of fish, because when you go into the water around an oil rig, you never know what size monster you might encounter.

My rig diving experience was in May, too early for the season, and bad weather had me grounded for almost an entire month before I finally made it out to the rigs. During this time I learned that Louisiana divers have become pretty good amateur oceanographers in their efforts to outguess the capricious weather and predict when and where they will find calm, clear water. Dan Nelson of Roland's Sporting Goods in New Orleans, and Jay Albeanese, Jr., Director of the Underwater Society of America, were the amateur oceanographers and spearfishermen who gambled with the rough water of the Gulf to take me out. They found clear water 60 miles from shore on a rig that was planted in 190 feet of water. This time I carried a camera instead of a spear gun and let Dan and Jay do the spearfishing.

Thirty years of diving in waters halfway around the world hadn't prepared me for the sight that met my eyes. I have never seen so many big fish concentrated in one small area. The water was crystal clear and I could see the structure of the entire rig, a huge maze of steel piping that plunged downward through the blue water until it disappeared in a haze 100 feet below. Circling around the outside and swarming through the rigging were thousands of fish of all kinds,

Amberjack beneath the oil rigs are so curious and unafraid they bump a photographer with their noses. (*Photo by Bill Barada*)

sizes and colors. Each group sought its own level and its own position, with schools of different kinds forming layers at various depths.
Floating lazily around the outside of the structure a few feet beneath the surface were hundreds of great barracuda, their gray-white
bodies drifting motionless with the current. Slightly below them and
moving fast, was a school of large cobia, their dark-brown, cigar-
shaped bodies wheeling and turning in perfect unison as they patrolled their selected beat. Deeper yet and continuing as far as I could
see, the water was alive with schools of amberjack and jack crevalle,
which circled around the rig as if drilling on parade. Inside the structure, swarming through the rigging as thick as women at a bargain
sale, were snapper, grouper, triggerfish, spadefish, bluefish and tropicals of all descriptions.

I was enthralled, hanging near the surface and drinking in the
sight, but Dan and Jay were already in action. Spearing a fish in
this giant aquarium was simply a matter of selecting the kind you
wanted and going after it. They ignored the amberjack and barracuda, drifting down after fish with more delicious-eating flesh. Dan
picked out a grouper in the 30-pound class which was hovering near
the edge of the rig about 60 feet down. Jay stayed near the surface
watching a school of cobia headed in his direction. I hung outside
the rig to watch the maneuvers. Dan's shot stoned the grouper and
after a couple of flips, it floated belly-up. He swam to a cross member,
sat astride it like a horse, tied the grouper off and began restringing
his gun.

Suspended motionless about ten feet outside the rig, I focused the
camera to snap a shot of Dan's fish. Then the amberjack started
giving me trouble. These were the most curious and unafraid fish I
had ever encountered in open water. They swirled around me so
close they blocked my vision and actually began bumping me with
their noses. At first I wasn't sure. I was concentrating on the camera
and felt a slight nudge against my back. I could see nothing but fish,
so thought it was my imagination and went back to my picture taking. Then I felt a series of bumps and nudges on all sides of my
body and looked down in time to see a 40-pound amberjack with
its nose against my stomach. I grabbed its tail. There was a split
second of wild commotion. Then the startled fish streaked away. Fish

must have a method of communication because they quit nosing me and I had no trouble getting my pictures.

I looked up just in time to see Jay Albeanese stick a large cobia. These fish are terrific fighters, almost as strong as amberjack, but their flesh is softer and a barb pulls out unless they are played carefully. The cobia streaked into the rigging with Jay following, swimming hard to reduce the tension of the line. In a game of follow-the-leader that was beautiful to watch, the fish weaved over, under and around cross members and piling with Jay right on its tail. The ride lasted less than a minute, but the fish was still giving Jay trouble when I finally caught up to them with the camera.

When I again saw Dan, he was working at the 80-foot level and had two more grouper tied off to the rigging. Amberjack had followed him down and were cruising back and forth just outside the rig. I remembered the nudging and tried to signal Dan to hang still so I could photograph the phenomena. He misunderstood my signal, leveled his gun, and shot the biggest of the group. I saw a flash of fish under the cross member, saw Dan jerked into a forward somersault, and they went flying straight down toward the bottom over 100 feet below. About 50 feet down, Dan's free hand grabbed a dangling cable and he stopped the rush with brute strength. He told me later that for a few minutes, it felt as if his arms were being pulled out of their sockets. The heavy exertion used up his remaining air and we surfaced to call it a day.

In two hours I had seen more big game fish than I had seen in thirty years of diving in other parts of the world. And this was not an exceptional day. Both Dan and Jay told me that later in the summer, when the water warmed up, there would be twice as many varieties and twice as many fish around the same rig, and that the same conditions existed around every structure in the gulf.

Dan Nelson examines the tangle a 30-pound amberjack has made of his riding rig during a wild battle beneath an offshore-oil rig. (*Photo by Bill Barada*)

The giant grouper, or jewfish, can be some of the easiest or the most difficult to approach, depending upon how spearwise they have become. (*Photo by Mick Church*)

10　Giants of the Reefs

JACK KIRK'S 100-foot *Velron* ploughed through the Pacific swells as if she enjoyed it, her high bow cutting the cresting waves and throwing a shower of spray and foam over the cabin windshield. We were four hours out in the Pacific and the slanting rays of the early-morning sun were bringing life and color to the blue water. San Clemente Island, 50 miles offshore, was only an indistinct dark blob on the horizon, but already sleepy-eyed divers were breaking out wet suits and inspecting the rigging on their guns. This was a special jewfish hunt and there were only a handful of us on board the big boat which normally carried a payload of 36 divers. A big fish hunt is definitely a case where too many divers spoil the broth and Jack, owner of the *Velron,* was running this trip for himself and a few friends. On board were Marty Pasos, an electronics engineer for North American Aviation and an avid big fish hunter; George Brauer, a skin-diving photographer who makes motion pictures for TV; and myself. Our goal was to shoot a movie for Brauer's TV show.

Our weapons were long, three-rubber guns, equipped with break-away rigging, and we were well prepared with extra harpoons, spearheads and line. Mine was the only gun on board without a powerhead attached to the shaft. This is a personal aversion, developed from sad experience with these devices. I don't know if it is coincidence, bad luck, or inferior equipment, but every powerhead I have used has given me nothing but trouble, and this trip proved to be no exception. My shaft was equipped with a straight 5-inch slip-tip head, and my theory is that if you can't get close enough to a fish to be sure this head will penetrate, don't shoot.

The giant sea bass of the Pacific is a different species from the jewfish of tropical waters. The Caribbean and Gulf jewfish live in caves and caverns of a reef and will stay in the same hole until dragged or chased out. Florida divers have spotted one in a cave while hunting small fish and had time to swim to shore, drive several miles to their home to pick up big spear guns, and return to find the jewfish still sitting in the same hole.

When hit with a spear, these big tropical fish wedge themselves into a cave and must be dragged out by brute force. Some Caribbean divers use a heavy line or cable from a boat to dislodge a speared jewfish. They attach a large hook to the line, swim into the cave and put the hook in the fish's gills, then throw the boat into gear and use the power of the motor to pull it out. These are extremely large and powerful fish (the official rod-and-reel record is 680 pounds), and underestimating their strength can get you into trouble. Jordan Klein, of Mako Products in Miami, tells of such an incident when a giant jewfish pulled his 16-foot outboard underwater.

Jordan and Frank Satanstein speared a mammoth jewfish which wedged itself into a cave. Additional free spears failed to kill it, so the divers used the boat to haul it out. Their mistake was in attaching the cable to the stern of the boat. When the monster sounded, it pulled the boat backward and swamped it. Jordan says it happened so fast, that one minute he was sitting in the boat—the next he was in the water, watching helplessly as his boat was towed underwater by the giant fish. It was headed toward a drop off on the edge of the Gulf Stream, and he had visions of his boat winding up in 6000 feet of water. Fortunately, the fish holed up after it had gone about

100 feet and Jordan was able to salvage both his boat and the jewfish. But he says this was undoubtedly the most expensive fish he ever speared.

The giant sea bass of the Pacific is slightly smaller than its tropical cousin (official record is 600 pounds), but it is just as powerful, and it is a free-swimming fish that doesn't hole up after it is hit. Pacific jewfish prowl the bottom from Monterey Bay to Baja California. They are always on the move, and migrate into shallow water when the temperature warms up in the spring and summer. Early June is their spawning season and there are more of them around at that

Mick Church, of the San Diego "Addicts" Club, with a 383-pound black sea bass which he speared while free diving off the Coronado Islands, just south of San Diego. (*Photo by Mick Church*)

time—usually in pairs. They feed on lobsters, crabs and bottom fish. Divers hunt them on rocky reefs and kelp beds along the mainland and offshore islands. Like other fish, jewfish seem to congregate in the same locations every year, and a diver who locates a hot jewfish spot is apt to keep it a secret from his best friend.

It was to one of these "secret" spots that Jack Kirk was heading, known only to a few divers—and every commercial fisherman on the coast.

The anchor plunged down through clear blue water to a rocky bottom 60 feet below. We were 100 yards off a mountainous, brush-covered section of the island, where the shoreline sloped sharply into very deep water. A strong current was running, so Jack, an old hand at skin-diving charters, lowered an outboard powered dinghy to tend the divers in case they hit a big fish or got into trouble. Jack stayed on board to insure the safety of his boat, and the rest of us donned scuba so we could stay on the bottom. An ocean current is almost always much weaker on the bottom than on the surface because the broken, rocky reef creates a drag that slows it down. If you come up downstream from your boat and still have air left in your tank, don't fight the current on the surface. Drop to the bottom, swim beyond the boat, and you can coast back without becoming exhausted.

Just as I was about to drop overboard, Jack noticed my gun and insisted that I use his powerhead. He claimed his was a new model, very dependable, and he wanted me to have every chance of getting a jewfish because they needed it for the movies. Marty Pasos and George Brauer agreed. They had the same models and were convinced all the "bugs" were ironed out. My objections were overcome and I used Jack's gun.

The water was exceptionally clear. George and Marty were 50 feet away and I could see the jumbled rocks and boulders of the steep slope another 30 feet beyond them. A sharp, high, clinking noise permeated the water like the sound of two pieces of metal banging together, and I assumed that something dangling from the boat was swinging in the current. No big fish were in sight, so I worked my way down the slope to a rock outcropping and lay quietly, watching for shadows or movement. Small fish darted in and out among the rocks and a school of yellowtail passed overhead, circling curiously around my exhaled bubbles. I saw Marty and George take stations about 60 feet away and also lie quietly watching the terrain.

The clinking sound persisted, a steady rhythmic ting, ting, ting, that had me puzzled. Then, down the slope at the misty edge of my range of vision, I saw two large black shadows. They were deep, at least 150 feet, and swimming parallel to shore. I watched them until they almost disappeared. Then two more came into view, moving up the slope at an angle toward our position. The first two turned and doubled back, this time headed above our spot, and I saw Marty start on an interception course. My eye caught another movement and I saw a huge jewfish circling from the opposite side and headed in my direction. It was amazing! I had never seen them act this way. The jewfish seemed to be converging on our position. I removed the safety on Jack's powerhead—checked the trigger safety on the gun, and moved slowly to meet the fish. I could see its eyeballs roll in my direction as I approached, but it stayed on course and passed about ten feet in front of me. These babies are so big that I guess the only thing they fear are sharks and killer whales. This one looked as if it would go about 300 pounds. I waited until it was going away, so the spear point would slide under its scales, aimed for a spot in back of its gills—and pulled the trigger. I felt my hand jerk as the shaft left the gun, saw it start toward the fish—then the powerhead fired prematurely and the harpoon stopped dead in the water. The uninjured jewfish continued to circle me as I gathered up the two tangled lines, one to the shaft and one to the barb on the powerhead, and swam back to the boat to reload—mentally cursing all powerheads and this one in particular.

George Brauer had missed his fish and was also on the boat restringing his gun. Marty had better luck. His powerhead worked beautifully and he had a big one on that was giving him a terrific ride. I could see him on the surface, his life vest inflated, and hanging to his breakaway float as the fish towed him through the water. Jack Kirk followed in the dinghy, ready to give Marty a hand as soon as the fish quieted down.

George Brauer saw my gun and offered me his spare. He claimed my accident was a freak. He owned a dive shop, sold hundreds of powerheads and they all worked perfectly. He guaranteed no misfires. Thinking that by this time the fish were probably spooked and difficult to approach, I agreed and went into the water with his powerhead.

The jewfish had disappeared. Except for the usual small fish, the bottom was empty. George was swimming close by and started banging on his tank with the butt of his gun. I thought he was in trouble, but he gave the O.K. signal and continued banging on his tank. The noise was similar to the one I had heard on the first dive and I suddenly realized why the jewfish had converged on our position. Many bottom fish such as ling cod, grouper, sheepshead and carp can be attracted by small noises underwater and the clinking that had puzzled me was Marty Pasos calling jewfish by tapping on his tank. I learned later that Marty had rigged up a special device which created the clinking sound when he pulled on a cord. I used my knife to bang my tank, and accompanied George in an underwater duet. In less than ten minutes the jewfish returned in force.

This time they didn't wander around looking for the source. They came directly at us from every direction, and soon a dozen or more were circling our position right under the boat. Some were real giants almost six feet long. I picked out the biggest, maneuvered into position, and fired. The shaft hit in back of the gills. I heard the powerhead explode, and the fish took off. Then, to my dismay, I saw my empty line and spear shaft trailing in the water. There was no tug or pull. It was as if I had used a spear without a barb. Investigation disclosed that the line to the barb of the powerhead was broken, and the barb was missing! Its velocity had broken the line, or cut it on the fish. Disgusted and sickened, I swam back to the boat after my own gun.

Marty was already hooked up on his second fish, and I had yet to get my first! I put on a fresh tank, grabbed my gun without a powerhead, and jumped back in the water. The jewfish were still under the boat, but excited and moving fast. Two big ones veered away before I got in range. Fish were all around me and I passed up several tempting opportunities as close as ten or fifteen feet. There had been more than enough boo-boos for one day, and I was determined to get close. Finally I saw a small 150-pounder swimming toward a large rock. I reversed direction so the rock would shield me from its

Ron Cox with a 300-pound giant grouper. Ben Cropp, the photographer, says they speared and captured it alive for Marineland of Australia, on the Gold Coast, Queensland, Australia. Ben says the grouper is still living in Marineland, and now weighs well over 350 pounds. (*Photo by Ben Cropp*)

view and, when the fish came by, it was only four feet away from my spear gun. The shaft penetrated deep—just behind the gills. The fish streaked off. I felt a tug as the breakaway released and watched the line pay out. Fifty feet away, the fish dived to the bottom and laid over on its side, as if stoned. The loose line was threaded around and through the sharp rocks which would cut it if the fish made another run. I had visions of losing another fish, and started collecting line and plucking it out of the rocks, hoping that the jewfish would hold still long enough for me to clear the line. The line was only half

Ben Cropp struggles upward with a 250-pound grouper he shot with a stand-ard spear gun at Nine Mile Reef, off Tweed Heads, New South Wales. Marks on the grouper are from dragging it out of a small cave 70 feet down. (*Photo by Eva Cropp*)

collected when I saw the fish's eyes roll, heard the thump of its tail, and it rushed right at me—almost knocking the gun out of my hands as it went by. A loop of line wrapped around my leg, another around my regulator, and I was dragged down the slope behind a frightened, 150-pound jewfish. I checked to make sure my knife was still in its scabbard, then began trying to work myself free. The fish was moving slowly but inexorably down the slope, and the line was taut as a bowstring. I grabbed the line and tried to pull. It slipped and I felt the heat of a rope burn through my leather gloves. Finally I managed to wrap the line around one hand and pulled in some slack. Then, with the other hand, managed to untangle the snarls. Once free of the fish, I started upward, letting the balance of the breakaway pay out as I swam. I was still ten feet from the surface when I hit the end of the 200-foot line, and I don't know which was the most tired—me or the jewfish. I squeezed the breakaway float to let its buoyancy give me a rest. I had worked harder to land that 150-pounder than I had on fish twice its size, taken while free diving.

Marty Pasos landed three jewfish that day, all between 300 and 400 pounds, and all with a powerhead. Many expert spearfishermen swear by these devices and use them consistently with excellent results. But I am still biased against powerheads and continue to use a straight detachable head, and try to get close.

Pacific coast jewfish are taken by free divers with the same equipment as with scuba. A few have been taken in shallow water, but they are usually 40 feet or deeper and require persistent, determined hunting just to see one. These fish take off like an express train when they are speared, and a long line, 200 to 300 feet, attached to your gun in a line pack or a reel, is an absolute necessity. Free divers work from a surface float such as an inner tube, surf mat or paddleboard, and a long line gives them a chance to get back to the surface and secure the fish to their float. Trying to dive with a line permanently attached to a surface float is not practical on the Pacific coast because it only gets tangled in the kelp. An inflatable float attached to the end of the breakaway is good insurance, because if all the line pays out, the float will usually bob to the surface after the fish slows down. If you prefer a reel, attach an inflatable float to the handle of your gun, and it may save both your gun and the fish if you are forced to let go.

Some divers recommend the use of a life vest to assist in fighting a big fish. It can be inflated underwater if a fish is holding you down, and on the surface its buoyancy helps prevent a fish from pulling you under. Other divers believe that an inflated life vest is a handicap in case you must dive quickly to untangle the line from kelp or rocks which could cause it to break. Practically all divers carry extra spear shafts on their float, and many carry an extra gun completely rigged. Hitting the fish with the extra gun gives you two lines in case the first one breaks or pulls out. The extra shafts are often armed with fixed cutting heads to administer the *coup de grâce* to a struggling fish.

Because Pacific coast jewfish are always on the move, you can spot them from the surface when the water is clear enough to see the bottom. They often swim in a zigzag pattern, and it is difficult to time your dive to intercept their path unless you can anticipate this pattern. Their progress is usually parallel to shore, and if you see one going away from you at an angle, don't try to follow. Swim parallel to shore in the direction the fish is traveling, and you may be in position to intercept when it returns.

A good way to locate "hot" jewfish spots, is to talk to commercial fishermen and abalone divers. They are closemouthed, but its easier to get them to talk than a spearfisherman who thinks you are competition.

An Indo-Pacific version of the jewfish, which Australian divers call the Queensland grouper, is one of the largest bony fish in the world, reported to reach lengths of 12 feet and weights of over 1000 pounds. Its characteristics are similar to Gulf and Caribbean species in that they seldom stray far from the cave in which they live. But these fish are more feared by native pearl divers than sharks. Divers who harvest the trochus shell will unhesitatingly enter shark-infested waters, but will not dive in an area where a Queensland grouper has been seen. Its fearful reputation is well earned, as it will stalk a diver as quietly and persistently as a cat stalks a mouse. These fish are highly prized by Australian divers, who hunt them in much the same manner as we hunt jewfish. But sometimes it is a question of who is stalking whom.

Bill Reichelt, an Australian spearfishing champion, tells of an en-

counter with two of these monsters which gave him a bad few moments. Bill told me he saw two large shapes swimming around a
ledge about 80-feet deep and dived to investigate what at first he
thought were porpoise. As he drew close, the two fish rose to meet
him and he saw they were Queensland grouper. Bill said that each
time he headed for one of the fish, the other would circle and move
in behind him. He finally had to surface without getting a shot. After
a brief rest, and a fresh supply of air in his lungs, he tried again.
This time the smaller fish rose first and Bill was able to plant a
spear in its side, before the other came up to box him in. Bill says,
"I streaked straight up to the surf ski (a diving paddleboard),
rammed my gun through the footstrap and called to my buddy, Ron
Cox. The fish hit the end of the line and the ski turned over and
went under. Ron gave me his gun and I followed the line down to
the fish. This time I was able to carefully place the spear in a vital
spot." By pulling on the two lines, Bill was able to haul the struggling fish toward the surface where it gave up. Most bottom fish,
when speared in deep water, are killed if pulled out of their normal
depth because the air in their body expands as the pressure is reduced.

The most prolific jewfish grounds in the world are the oil rigs in
the Gulf of Mexico. These monsters congregate under the rigs during June, July and August, and skin divers use the same riding rigs
and the same techniques on them as they do on open-water fish,
(as described in Chapter 7). The jewfish hide in a muddy layer of
water that always hangs ten to fifteen feet above the bottom and a
diver riding a jewfish under the rigs not only must dodge the maze
of pilings, cross members and risers of the structure, he also faces
the hazards of black water and a junkyard of machinery, pipes, cable and wire discarded during construction.

Burr Tettleton and Farley Sonnier introduced me to their version
of Louisiana jewfish busting. Burr is a geologist for Mobil Oil Cor-
poration in Shreveport, Louisiana, and was doing a survey of the
ecology of the rigs for his company. Farley is a lawyer in Lake
Charles, Louisiana, who is as meticulous about spearfishing as he is
in preparing a brief. The first rig we hit was 60 miles from shore in
90 feet of water. Burr and Farley went overboard with spear guns

and I followed with two Nikonos cameras dangling from my neck. My assignment was to shoot pictures of rig spearfishing for an article in *Skin Diver* magazine and I needed both color and black-and-white photos. One camera was equipped with a Hydrostrobe flash gun and loaded with Ektachrome-X color film. The other, without flash, was loaded with Tri-X which is fast enough to shoot in natural light. Burr and Farley made a fast survey of the rig, swimming just above the murky layer to see if they could flush a jewfish. Burr had told me that these fish will often swim up out of the murk to look you over, then swim back down and lie on the bottom.

He spotted a big warsaw grouper and went after it. The fish was lying quietly, and as Burr approached, it moved off slowly, making no attempt to escape or bolt. The fish was almost half the length of Burr's body and about two feet thick. I estimated its weight at well over 60 pounds. Burr closed slowly until he was less than six feet away, then I heard the twang of his spear gun and saw the shaft hit in back of the gills—too high for a kill shot. The next few moments were a blur of action as the fish dragged Burr in a wild ride through the rigging. It zigzagged around piling, over and under cross members and dived through cable and debris with Burr following and dodging obstructions like a water skier on a slalom course. The ride was over in two minutes, but every second was packed with thrills that few sports can equal. When it was finally subdued, and Burr was hauling it to the surface, I tapped him on the shoulder and signaled for him to stop for a picture. He had a frantic look in his eyes, shook his head violently negative and continued on to the surface. On board the boat he explained that he was out of air and couldn't signal because both hands were full of fish, cable and spear gun. His warsaw weighed out at 70 pounds and was a 1968 record for that species, among members of the Southwest Council of Diving Clubs.

We ran into jewfish on the next rig but, of course, nobody had a spear gun. We got all the fish we wanted on the first rig, and convinced that May was too early for jewfish, Burr took his camera in the water instead of a gun and Farley stayed on board. We fooled around shooting pictures of tiny tropicals until we were almost out

Riding a big fish beneath the offshore-oil rigs means being towed in a wild merry-go-round through pilings, stanchions and cross members. A 70-pound warsaw grouper in the bottom left-hand corner of this photo has Burr Tettleton spinning in a tight circle. (*Photo by Bill Barada*)

of air. Then, at the 90-foot level, I saw Burr wave his arm wildly and point toward the bottom 30 feet below. I looked down and the reason for his excitement became apparent. A huge jewfish was coming slowly up out of the haze. It was swimming vertically, parallel to a riser, and directly toward Burr who was working frantically with his camera trying to adjust the focus and aperture. The fish swam by me so close that a manilla leader dangling from its mouth came within reach and I couldn't resist the temptation to grab it. The heavy line was rotten and broke immediately, or I may have experienced a ride of my own. My action disturbed the fish and it began weaving in and out through the rigging as if trying to conceal its huge body behind the 30-inch pilings. From its length and girth, I estimated its weight to be around 300 pounds.

We were almost out of bottom time and our tanks were nearly empty, so we contented ourselves with shooting the fish with cameras instead of going back to the boat for spear guns. I wanted a close-up shot, head on, and concentrated upon maneuvering the fish into position. Finally, on the bottom, it swam behind a cluster of rigging. I reversed direction, slipped around the piling and met it head on. The flash went off about two feet from its partially open mouth. That was the most surprised jewfish I have ever seen.

The fish swam off, and when my eyes adjusted to the surroundings, I couldn't believe what I saw. All around me, their huge bulks partially obscured in the haze, were at least six or seven jewfish, and each one looked almost twice as big as the one I had been stalking. Burr tapped me on the shoulder, signaled he was out of air and we headed reluctantly back toward the surface. When told about the jewfish, Farley looked dismayed. He checked the wind and time and said, disgustedly, "No more today. We've got to head back." Then,

Burr Tettleton fights his way to the surface from 125 feet down after an exhausting ride through the oil structure. His fish weighed in at 70 pounds, a record warsaw grouper for 1968. (*Photo by Bill Barada*)

with a puzzled expression, he said, "Jewfish are not supposed to be there this time of year!"

Jewfish and grouper of tropical waters like to live in coral or rocky reefs that are honeycombed with large caverns and cracks. Occasionally they will be found on a smooth, sloping bottom, but a better place to hunt is along the face or bottom of a steep wall that drops into 50 feet of water or deeper. Look for an underwater cave-in, or a jumble of boulders, under which big fish can hide. Often they will be seen sitting motionless in the open, waiting to ambush any unwary fish that swim within range of their cavernous mouths. Some species of grouper can change their color to blend with their surroundings and are so well camouflaged that you can look right at a 100-pound fish and not see it. This is why it pays to move very slowly, especially as you come over the top of a reef or ledge with a sandy bottom below. Look for rocks or bumps in the sand that are shaped like a fish, and examine them for a telltale fin, tail or eye that will bring the fish into focus.

Cave-dwelling fish that reach 100 pounds and more, such as snapper, grouper and jewfish, can be the easiest fish in the ocean to approach and spear, or they can be the most skittish. It depends upon how often they have been hunted, and how spearwise they have become. Popular diving spots, such as the Florida Keys and the Bahamas, have been worked so hard by so many skin divers that any big fish that haven't been frightened away or speared, run for a hole or deep water the moment they see a skin diver. In virgin territory, where the fish are unaccustomed to human predators, they are unafraid and you can approach the big ones without difficulty. The first time I visited Guaymas, Mexico, in 1943, I counted twelve, 100-pound-plus jewfish and grouper milling around a single ledge, and several swam out to meet me. I dived the area in 1968, and saw five 50-pounders in three days of diving. They were so spooky that I used every trick in the book to get a shot at one of them.

If a grouper or jewfish runs into a hole that is a dead-end cave, you can follow and shoot it. But a spearwise fish will pick out a succession of tunnels with a multitude of entrances and exits. A big fish, speared in such a maze, will hopelessly tangle or break your line. Occasionally, they will streak out another entrance and you wind up with your line threaded through the reef, with a fish struggling in the open on the other side. When hunting cave-dwelling fish, most divers prefer a short, heavy line of flexible stainless steel cable, and they try to pull the fish into the open while it is still stunned from the impact. Experts with the Hawaiian sling don't use a line at all. They carry a lot of extra shafts and put enough free spears in the fish to kill it or quiet it down so it can be manhandled. For a while I used a small, collapsible parachute to stop the rush of a big fish before it could swim into a hole. A spring-loaded pilot parachute was attached to a short harpoon line and tucked into a breakaway canister. When I hit a fish big enough to release the breakaway, the parachute popped out and put a drag on the fish that stopped its rush within a very short distance. My first chance to try it was at Puerto Penasco in Baja California, and it worked even better than I had hoped.

A flock of diving sea birds led Homer Lockwood and me to a huge school of bait that had been driven into a shallow cove. The small fish were so closely packed, they formed a flexible tunnel around me, with ends that opened and closed as I passed. The wall

Grouper and jewfish, that are skittish and difficult to approach in daylight, often sleep at night, and are so docile a diver with a light can touch them with his hands. This grouper was photographed at night in a cave in the Bahamas. (*Photo by Mick Church*)

of bait extended all the way to the bottom and turned the water so
dark it took several seconds for my eyes to adjust to the dim light.
When objects came into focus, the head of a large grouper was facing me, no more than six feet away. My startled recognition spooked
the fish and it bolted before I could level the gun. Bait fish were
swirling about me so thick it was the same as looking through the
smoke of a forest fire. Then the heads of more grouper appeared,
all facing me from the same distance, forming a ring of big fish
which completely encircled me. I was so astounded that I stared at
each fish until it bolted and I had to surface for air without firing a
shot.

On the next dive, I was looking down the barrel of the gun as my
eyes adjusted. The instant I saw a fish I fired. I felt a jerk as the
parachute popped out and disappeared. The breakaway line started
to pay out, then went slack and I thought I had lost the fish. On the
surface, I started to retrieve the line and felt the weight of the fish
still struggling and fighting. The fish weighed 60 pounds, but I towed
it to the boat as easily as a 20-pounder. All I had to do was keep a
tension on the line and the opening and closing of the parachute
fought the fish for me.

I thought the parachute was the perfect technique for fighting big
fish and recommended it to all of my friends. Then one day I hit a
200-pounder that caused me to change my mind. This larger fish
charged away with such power, it tore the parachute to shreds. I discarded the parachute idea and apologized to my friends.

The big game fish of skin divers along the North Atlantic coast is
the striped bass which reaches weights well over 100 pounds. These
fish are legal for spearfishing in some states, but protected by law
in others. The striped bass is a free-swimming fish found in shallow
water near shore, often in the surf or just outside the surf line, in
water from five to twenty feet deep. Like salmon, they migrate up
streams to spawn, and heavy concentrations are found in spring and
summer around the entrance to rivers and bays. Skin divers hunt
them along rocky shorelines and jetties in the same areas in which
they look for toutog. Frank Xedus says he finds them most frequently when the water is rough, and around points where the current is strong. Like other free-swimming reef fish, stripers are usually

near the bottom, and Frank says to look for them close to or between the rocks.

Striper hunting is in dirty water which makes long-range guns useless. The best weapon is a short, powerful gun equipped with a detachable head. Frank says, "If I get a head shot, or just in back of the gills, I figure I've got him, but sometimes a body shot will do. A belly or tail shot will probably lose the fish. I have found no sure way of landing one after it is hit except to try and get my hands in its gills. Even then, I pray a little because they are strong fighters and their flesh is tender so a spearhead will not always hold."

Striper hunting is limited to the summer months, not only because of the freezing weather, but because the fish move into deep water and hunting is poor even if a diver can tolerate the cold.

Another giant of the reefs is the giant sea turtle which is found in the same area as grouper and jewfish and few divers can resist the temptation to grab one and go for a ride. Spearing them is considered beneath the dignity of a skin diver, and the real sport is in catching them with your hands. They are found sleeping on the bottom, or free swimming over the reefs. You should always approach a turtle from the side, rear or the top so you can grasp the shell with both hands and avoid the possibility of a nasty bite from its powerful jaws. Grab the shell with one hand in back of its head and the other near its tail. Use the hand on the tail as a lever to turn the turtle in the direction you wish to go. Small turtles, no more than three feet long, are easy to handle and do not swim strongly enough to give you a good ride. But a big one, four to five feet long, is very powerful and it takes a lot of strength to turn it toward the surface.

The largest and strongest turtle I ever tackled was off Cozumel Island in the Mexican Caribbean. We were free diving near a barrier reef that dropped off to a sandy bottom 80 feet below. I spotted a large turtle cruising toward the reef, handed my camera to a companion and dived. It was so huge that my hands could barely span its shell. The instant I exerted pressure, the turtle sounded and headed out to sea, towing me through the water at a clip faster than a man could swim. I levered my body forward, braced my arms, and put every ounce of strength I could muster in an attempt to turn its head toward the surface. I was about to give up when the turtle

Ron Church subdues a grouper by grabbing it in the eye sockets. (*Photo by Mick Church*)

Joyce Irwin takes a wild, fast ride on a 200-pound green sea turtle off Isla Mujeres, Mexico. (*Photo by Mick Church*)

Paul Knight boats a 25-pound striper speared off Shinnecock Inlet, New York. (*Photo courtesy of Voit Rubber Co.*)

gradually began to give ground and we started a long, slow arc upward. My head broke into the air just long enough for me to gulp a couple of breaths, spit out my snorkel and call for my companions to help. Then the turtle pulled me under and we did it all over again. Spitting out the snorkel was a mistake. My arms ached from the exertion and I was gasping for air. Without a snorkel, every breath seemed to coincide with a wave that broke over my head and I inhaled as much water as air. The turtle seemed to be getting stronger, and finally dragged me so deep that I was forced to let go. I asked the Mexican divers why they didn't help and one of them showed me a piece bitten out of his bathing suit. The turtle and I were threshing around so violently that every time they tried to move in, its head swung in their direction and its gnashing beak kept them at a distance.

Turtle meat is delicious. It tastes like chicken or rabbit, and can be eaten as steak, roast, stew or soup. That huge *tortuga blanca* would have made a lot of turtle steak and I hated to let it go.

Riding giant turtles and mantas or spearing grouper, jewfish and other giants of the reefs should only be attempted by divers who have the confidence and watermanship that comes with experience. Although these animals are not considered predators and can be approached safely with little or no danger of attack, they are large enough and strong enough to test the skills and physical stamina of experts and a diver who is not completely at home in the underwater environment could be drawn into situations beyond his limitations. This is even more true of hunting for predators and denizens such as sharks, barracuda, eels, etc., which present the added danger of possible attack.

Author Barada subdues a small shark speared off Panama City, Florida. (*Photo by Bill Barada*)

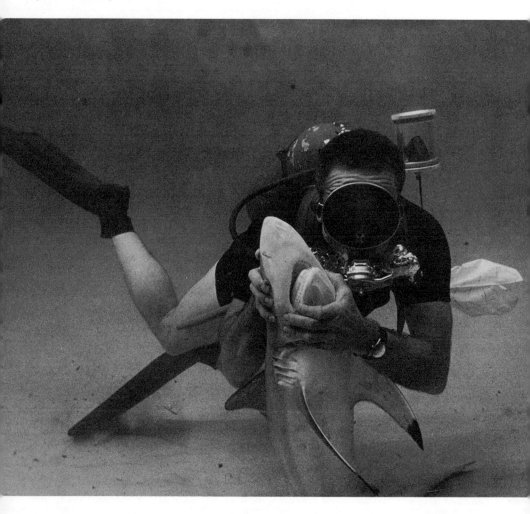

We were at Rangiroa atoll in the Tuamotu Islands of French Polynesia and the narrow strip of water in this pass, only 300 yards wide, a mile long and 80 feet deep, probably has more sharks per cubic foot of water than any place in the world. My companions were Dewey Bergman, of See and Sea Holidays in San Francisco, and Al Giddings of the Bamboo Reef Dive Shop in the same city. Dewey and Al each carried 16mm. motion-picture cameras encased in metal housings, to capture the shark action. I was the "bait," assigned the task of spearing a fish to trigger the sharks into a frenzy. This was our fourth day of diving with the sharks and we had filmed over 2000 feet of sharks in different stages in a feeding frenzy. But the most spectacular scene had so far escaped the cameras. The action we wanted was of the sharks fighting each other for a speared fish. We had witnessed it many times as they formed into a pack, spiraling through the water at tremendous speeds after the lead shark with the fish, fighting each other like mad. The pack action was always out of camera range, after a shark had broken a spear-gun line. This time we were trying again, and Dewey carried an extra gun.

We worked our way slowly down the face of the cliff, belly-tight against the coral, and into a shallow cave at 40 feet. Hundreds of sharks schooled above, below and around us. Groups of two and three patrolled slowly back and forth in front of our cave, so close I could see their eyes roll as they passed. Al was far left, Dewey next to me, I leveled the spear gun waiting for a fish to swim directly in front of Al and Dewey's cameras. The sharks got more excited, swimming faster in circles, and always their eyes watching us. I shot a parrot fish. It dived for the coral, landed three feet in front of Dewey's camera, and all hell broke loose. Sharks pounced on it from every direction, lightning fast, the drumming of their tails rumbling in our ears. Dewey and Al filmed like mad. A shark grabbed the fish and took off, others after it. One zoomed right at Al's head, mouth open, teeth bared. He shoved the camera at it and yelled, it veered off. I was dragged into the open, grabbed for coral and missed, the pull was terrific. Sharks were everywhere, zooming in on the fish, all around me, bunching up and fighting each other. I let the gun go and the shark streaked for the surface. The pack followed, two right on

its back, three more on top of them, five or six more close behind
and the rest following, bumping and biting. One broke the surface in
a boil of foam. Then the fight was over and the pack broke up,
leaving the wooden spear gun floating on the surface, the shaft dangling in the water from the end of the line.

Hundreds of sharks were still gyrating through the water, but less
frantically and at much slower speeds. Dewey handed me the extra
spear gun and led the way down the cliff to a wide ledge near the
bottom. He settled into a shallow ditch about three feet deep which
provided a wider scope for the cameras, but less protection from
the sharks. Al found another foxhole about 20 feet to our left. I
was in the open looking for a slot between them. A shark cruised
two feet above Al's head. He ducked, aimed the camera and I heard
its motor whine. Two more passed close to Dewey, their bellies almost rubbing the coral. Something moved behind me and I looked

Dewey Bergman and Al Giddings with the motion-picture cameras they used
to film our shark action in Tahiti. Dewey is using a Bell and Howell 16mm.
camera in a Jon Hall housing. Al's camera and housing are of his own design
and manufacture, complete with underwater lights. (*Photo by Bill Barada*)

Sharks in groups of 2 and 3 patrolled slowly back and forth, so close we could see their eyes roll as they passed. (*Photo by Bill Barada*)

Hundreds of sharks were gyrating through the water, very excited and moving fast. (*Photo by Bill Barada*)

down on the back of an eight-foot gray that almost brushed my legs. I scrambled into Dewey's foxhole.

Al pointed toward the surface. The Tahitian spear gun was floating almost directly overhead. Suddenly a shark zoomed at it. Starting from the bottom, 70 feet deep, it shot straight up, like a torpedo, moving so fast it jumped clear out of the water. We heard the splash. Others followed, rocketing vertically at tremendous speed, hitting the gun, their momentum hurtling them out of the water. We watched fascinated, and a sudden thought sent fingers of cold fear through my veins. What if a diver had been holding that gun, snorkeling on the surface? We had speculated on trying this with a fish on the end of the spear so we could film the attack. It might have been a fatal mistake. We will never know. (Later, natives on shore nearby told us that they saw the sharks breaking the surface, boiling the water to a froth, and were sure we had been eaten alive.)

I leveled the spear gun, waiting for a fish to swim between Dewey and Al. It was a double-rubber arbalete that felt like a popgun when I looked at the sharks. I thought of the powerhead on shore loaded with a shotgun shell that exploded on impact. We had left it because in the frenetic excitement of a feeding frenzy, things happened so fast we only had time for the cameras and spear gun. Killing one shark out of the hundreds around us would do no good, and a loaded powerhead would be dangerous to handle in the confusion.

Fish were all around us. Snapper, parrots and tang passed inches in front of the sharks' mouths, but they never made a pass except when a fish was wounded or impaled on a spear, then they went wild. I aimed at a 15-pound snapper and a big gray immediately lined up behind it. I could see the shark's eyes roll, waiting for me to shoot.

I hit the fish solid in the head. It darted away. I felt a jerk as it hit the end of the line, and I grabbed the coral with my free hand. A drumming roar filled my ears as hundreds of sharks rocketed toward the fish. Blurred gray shapes streaked past me within inches. A shark grabbed the fish on the run, it jerked out of its mouth, the gray whipped into an Immelman turn, its mouth open. I felt the line grow taut as the big gray grabbed the fish, a dozen others on its back and more coming. I watched hypnotized, as the flying wedge of 40 or 50 snapping, twisting bodies hurtled in a mad merry-go-round at the end of my ten-foot line. It was all I could do to hold on. Then, horrified, I saw Dewey directly in their path. Intent on filming, he had floated up out of the slot. The pack roared over him, blotting him from view as they flew past. Dewey, unharmed, quickly scrambled back to cover. Al was bobbing like a jack-in-the-box trying to film while ducking sharks. They came from everywhere, tails lashing, they moved like greased lightning, zipping into the melee with open mouths and flashing teeth. Great gashes and cuts opened on their sides and bellies in front of our eyes. I felt the coral break under my grip; I was being dragged into the open, into the pack. I let the gun go and watched the battling horde streak away and disappear into the mist. The familiar silence of the underwater world was a welcome relief, like the quiet after a pitched battle.

I felt a peculiar exhilaration never before experienced. We looked at each other and I could tell that Al and Dewey felt the same way, a high feeling of invulnerability and accomplishment as if nothing could hurt us. We were drunk with excitement. We moved together out across the smooth bottom of the pass. There were no caves, cuts or crevices to offer even a token of protection, but we were unconcerned. The sharks had never come at us except when they were baited or we had speared a fish. Both spear guns were gone and the powerhead was on shore. All we had were the cameras and our knives. I laughed to myself at the thought of fighting these sharks with a knife. They moved so fast and so erratically in a frenzy that even a powerhead would be almost useless.

Suddenly, out of nowhere and for no reason, sharks were all around us again. They were still excited, moving fast, their eyes rolling, tails lashing and opening and closing their mouths. We could see their teeth and hear their jaws gnashing. Sickening fingers of fear clutched at my stomach. Their actions were different, definitely aggressive, making unmistakable passes, coming directly at us and not turning until they were a foot or two away. It's an eerie feeling to look directly into a shark's eyes two feet away and watch its eyes roll from side to side, and its teeth flash as if debating whether to bite or not. Cold shivers ran over my back and my scalp tingled with fright. There were at least 100 sharks in the school, and it was impossible to follow all of the action. We were only three or four

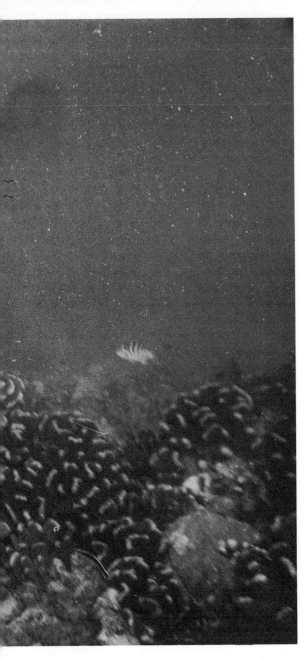

Suddenly, out of nowhere, sharks were all around us again, their eyes rolling, tails lashing, and their mouths opening and closing. (*Photo by Bill Barada*)

feet apart, but sharks were shooting between us, around our legs and in back of our heads. I could hear Dewey's camera running, but he was not watching where it was pointing. He couldn't miss, the water was thick with sharks, frenzied, darting in and out from all angles. I thought, "We've pushed our luck too far. One will strike and it will be all over. They'll be on us the way they went after the fish."

There was no place to go. The wall of the pass was 100 yards away through a swirl of angry, excited sharks. It may as well have been a mile. I felt naked and exposed, with only the tiny Calypso camera in my hands. A curious, fatalistic calm swept over me. I relaxed and breathed easily. Al must have had the same feeling. I saw his arms go limp, his huge motion-picture camera hanging at his side, his eyes sweeping over the gyrating sharks in an attitude that seemed to say, "What in the hell are we doing here?"

A big gray went into the classic attack pattern, dropped its dorsal fins, arched its back, body quivering, teeth snapping. Then it came at me, zigzagging like a streak of light. I snapped the shutter as it veered off, inches over my head. Others started the same pattern. I signaled Dewey, "Let's get out!" Dewey signaled Al. We put our backs together, tight, and began "walking" toward the wall of the pass, feet downward on the bottom so our flippers wouldn't invite attack. The sharks followed, darting at us from all angles, so close we could touch them. We moved slowly, and it seemed to take hours before we reached the base of the cliff and began to work our way up the wall. Part way up, the action slowed to a mild frenzy. There was time to look around and take stock between passes. I began to relax a little and think, "Maybe we will get out of this yet!" We moved up the wall, crawling, slipping, belly-down, watching our feet. Halfway up, the action slowed to normal, with only a few sharks swimming around, staying ten to fifteen feet away. Ten feet from the surface our worries were over and we used our decompression time to photograph colorful reef fish and coral formations, confident that the sharks would stay in deep water below the wall.

Discussing it later, we all agreed that we were within seconds of sudden death while we were in the open. We also agreed that the aggressive action of the sharks was completely unexpected and took us by surprise. We had been in the pass several times, without spear-

Ben Cropp, Australian spearfishing champion, and sharks killed with an explosive powerhead. One is 9 feet long, the other 6 feet. (*Photo by Eva Cropp*)

Until man invaded their domain, sharks had everything their own way. Now, armed with explosive powerheads, man is the aggressor, actively hunting and stalking this hated enemy underwater. (*Photo courtesy of Oceanic Equipment Corp. Inc.*)

ing fish, and the sharks had shown only a mild curiosity, never anything like we had just experienced. Al suggested that the pass was a spawning ground and that we had inadvertently ventured too close to a "nesting" place. Dewey said the pass is always full of sharks, all year, and that they were just excited from all of the diving and spearfishing we had been doing for the past few days. I compare it to the signs at Yellowstone National Park warning tourists, "Don't feed the bears." Trouble usually comes when a tourist quits feeding the bears, and we had quit feeding the sharks. But who knows?

Dewey and Al's motion picture, *The Predators,* has such hair-raising sequences of shark feeding that even veteran skin divers shudder when they view it. At the 1967 International Underwater Film

Festival in Santa Monica, California in which it won a gold medal, I was sitting next to some Australian divers while *The Predators* was being shown and heard one of them say, "Good grief, I've never seen so many sharks, any place." This diver was one of the stars of an Australian shark-hunting film which was shown previously. Jim Stewart, Chief Diver for Scripps Institute of Oceanography at La Jolla, California, was watching the film in San Diego and told me, "You guys were just plain crazy." Jim was attacked by a gray near Wake Island and knows what it's like to see a shark go into its pre-attack shivers. Our venture was not backed by a government grant and the expedition was not staffed by a retinue of famous scientists, but its value to the study of shark-behavior patterns cannot be denied. Members of the Shark Research Panel of the Smithsonian Institute were unanimous in their acclaim and said it had taught them a great deal.

Every audience I have talked to about skin diving, whether it is one person or 2000, has invariably asked about the danger of sharks. After more than 30 years of personal experience and talking to thousands of other divers throughout the world, I still don't know what they will do—and am convinced that nobody else does—including the sharks. All of the books, scientific experiments and experience of divers attest that swimming among a school of sharks in a feeding frenzy is tantamount to suicide. These same sources state that spearing fish when sharks are present, or swimming while you are wounded and bleeding, is inviting attack. The three of us, bleeding from fresh coral cuts, dived and speared fish amidst hundreds of man-killers in a feeding frenzy for four consecutive days and were not attacked. Yet, the next man to try it may be ripped to pieces. And single, isolated grays have attacked divers who were minding their own business.

I am convinced that sharks are completely unpredictable. I am also convinced that the danger of attack is overrated, and our fears are exaggerated. They abound in all the oceans from the arctic to the tropics, and are prevalent off all the sea coasts of the world. If sharks actively sought out human victims, swimming, water skiing, surfing and skin diving in the ocean would be impossible. The truth is that you are in more danger while walking the streets or playing golf than while swimming because fifty times as many people are struck by lightning as are attacked by sharks. And skin divers kill more sharks every day than the total of shark attacks on divers in the 30 years I have been going underwater.

Sharks have made little evolutionary change in the 300 million years they have terrorized the sea. Until man invaded their domain they had everything their own way. Now, armed with powerful spear guns and powerheads, man is the aggressor, actively hunting and stalking this hated enemy in its own grounds, underwater.

Many stories describe sharks as cannibals which attack and devour a wounded member of the pack as readily as they do a wounded fish. This may be true under special circumstances or with a particular species, but my experience and the experiences of other divers indicate that it is a rare exception rather than a common occurrence. Dewey Bergman, who accompanied Dr. Perry Gilbert during his shark experiments in the Tuamotu Islands, said the sharks they killed in Rangiroa Pass were ignored by the pack. Also, Australian divers, Ron Taylor and Ben Cropp, have produced several motion pictures of divers killing sharks while using spears armed with explosive powerheads and the wounded sharks were never attacked by others swimming nearby. A number of divers hunt sharks for sport off the Florida Keys and none have reported witnessing cannibalistic action. There is little doubt that the explosion and blood in the water attract sharks into the area, but the sharks only attack each other when fighting over a wounded fish.

Not all sharks are dangerous. There are 250 different species, many of which lie sleeping in the sand or rocks, and are so sluggish that they can be bumped and nudged without disturbing their rest. Small versions of these, such as swell sharks, horned sharks, leopards, angels, etc., can be grabbed by the tail and wrestled to the surface by hand. They are not considered a challenge, and are seldom speared by experienced hunters. The great, free-swimming man-eaters such as whites, hammerheads, tigers, makos and grays are another story, and hunting them is one of the most exciting sports a diver can practice. Some of these are monsters of unbelievable size. The great white is the largest, growing to lengths of 35 feet and weights of 7000 pounds. The tiger is second, growing to 30 feet and weighing more than 4000 pounds. Hammerheads and makos go over 12 feet and weigh more than 1000 pounds. The rest are more slender, or

Not all sharks are dangerous. The sluggish nurse shark found sleeping on the bottom can be approached with impunity. (*Photo by Mick Church*)

smaller and seldom weigh more than 500 pounds. These are dangerous antagonists which have the ability to dispatch a skin diver with
a single bite. But, as with other wild animals, of superior physical
ability, man has the advantage because he is more aggressive and
has the brain to devise weapons that make up for his puny strength
and poor swimming.

Moderate-sized sharks can be speared and landed with the same
equipment that is used for hunting extremely large fish. But this is
dangerous because sharks are tough and extremely difficult to kill.
I have never seen a shark deliberately turn on its attacker. But they
fight the spear, and their wild gyrations may bring their snapping
jaws in your direction. A much more efficient and safer method of
hunting large sharks is with an explosive head that blows a large hole
through the shark's body and usually kills it instantly. A powerful
spear gun or hand spear is not required with powerheads because
only a moderate impact will trigger the explosive charge. These are
usually for defense and are used extensively by some commercial divers when working in shark-infested waters. Jerry Turner of Miami,
Florida is a commercial diver who believes that offense is the best defense where sharks are concerned.

Jerry told me, "The use of explosives underwater is a great attrac-
tion for sharks. They appear almost immediately, and you will always
kill a multitude of fish on the first blast. The sharks are no trouble as
long as the fish last, then they eyeball the divers. On no occasion have
I ever seen a shark make a lightning attack. They are slow and make
a thorough recon around you before making up their minds. If
there is blood in the water, they get giddy and shake and shimmy all
over before making a pass at you. It is easy to spot one that is ready by
his fast action of shakes and quivers. I have used the Bang Stick on
sharks when they get the shimmies. I just can't wait for them to get
set. I don't stay in the water that sharks are in, but I have tagged several before they could make up their minds as to what they wanted to
do. I have found that it is best to charge them if you can't get out of
the water immediately. It seems to shake them up no end. They have
always had their way and when something gets after them, they seem
to crack up. This gives you time to get out of the water."

Jerry's advice is sound and you should get out of the water when

sharks are around. It's true that hundreds of thousands of divers swim
in shark-infested waters every day and the odds against attack are
more than 1000 to 1, but remember they are completely unpredictable and you never know what the particular shark you are looking
at will do. This has been demonstrated over and over again by experiments with shark repellents. Various chemicals and bubble screens
seem to be effective for a while, then a single shark breaks through
and the entire pack swarms into the repellent as if it were non-exist-
ent. One diver thought he had the answer in a rod which delivered a
sharp electric shock when it touched a shark. Early experiments were
highly successful and sharks hit with the shock streaked away in
panic. But, during an experiment on a docile shark in Florida's Sea-
quarium, the shock made the shark so angry it turned on the diver
and he was lucky to get out of the water alive. So, unless you like to
live dangerously and are willing to gamble that a shark won't bite,
get out of the water when one comes around. Don't move fast or try
to run, as this is more apt to encourage an attack. Keep your eyes on
the shark and move slowly toward your boat or shore.

Almost every time you dive in tropical waters, you will see great
barracuda, gray ghosts three to six feet long, drifting silently near the
surface. Often they will stalk a diver or pass very close, jaws opening
and closing and teeth snapping. For years barracuda had a reputation
as vicious man-killers on a par with sharks, but experience has proved
that they are only big fish with sharp teeth, and there is little danger
of unprovoked attack. The teeth gnashing is not a threatening ges-
ture, but a method of pumping water through the fish's gills so it can
breathe. However, they strike like lightning at a bright, flashing object or a speared fish, and when barracuda are around, it pays to
move with calculated slowness and keep your eyes open while retriev-
ing a speared fish. They are considered fair game for underwater
hunters who enjoy a dash of danger with their sport. The flesh is not
especially tasty, and they are hunted primarily as predators. Florida
divers take them with a free spear from a Hawaiian sling, others use
the same conventional weapons as when spearing any large pelagic
fish. Keep in mind that they move like a streak of light and their razor-sharp teeth can slice a large chunk out of your body with a single
bite. Always try to hit a barracuda in the head or solid portion of its

The safest spot to spear a moray eel is in the head, and with a hand spear long enough to hold it away from you. Ray Hoglund tangles with a big one off Marathon, Florida. (*Photo by Paul Tzimoulis*)

body that will slow its swimming, otherwise its erratic rushes may bring its snapping teeth too close for safety.

The moray eel is one of the most maligned sea creatures a diver will encounter. Like huge snakes with powerful jaws and sharp teeth, they grow to lengths of more than six feet and infest the same crevices and caves of tropical and Pacific coast reefs inhabited by lobsters. I have never heard of an unprovoked attack by a moray, but a number of friends have had their fingers ripped to the bone while they were trying to dig a lobster out of a hole, and grabbed an eel by mistake. I have never seen anything more vicious than injured moray. They go berserk, biting at everything within reach of their mouths, including themselves. A hooked moray can break a 60-pound-test fishing line by sliding its supple, powerful body into a half hitch and pulling against its own muscles. Two fishermen hauled one into a rowboat and its attack was so vicious, both men left the boat and dived into the water. A moray's muscles are so strong that when speared, it can twist the ¼-inch tines of a frog gig into a pretzel, and I've seen them bite a metal shaft so hard their teeth crack like popcorn. On the other hand, I, and hundreds of other divers, have fed morays by hand, and I have bumped their noses with the back of my hand or knife to drive them away from abalone without any of us being bitten.

Eels and lobsters must have a sort of non-aggression pact or agreement because they often inhabit the same holes, and a west coast diver who is afraid to put his hand near an eel doesn't get any lobsters. A diver peering into a hole and waiting for his eyes to adjust to the darkness, is often startled to see the open mouth and vicious head of a moray staring at him a few inches from his mask. The trick is to move very slowly and deliberately, with no quick motions of your hands or arms, until you are ready to grab the lobster. Never make a fast grab past an eel's head. Come in from the opposite side and pin the lobster against the rocks or coral. This method has allowed me to take four or five lobsters out of a hole with a dozen morays dangling from the ceiling and even pull lobsters out of an abandoned trap with two huge eels coiled inside.

Spearing a moray is easy because you can get so close it is impossible to miss, but landing one may cause you trouble. Never spear an eel unless you can hit it in the head or just in back of the head, so you can control the action of its jaws. A five-tine hand spear or a fixed head on a solid shaft is best because a line or cable on a detachable head gives the eel too much freedom of movement. The most dangerous time is when removing the spear. Morays are extremely difficult to kill and may turn on you once they are free. The safest way is to use your knife, or other instrument, to break their jaw before taking them off the spear.

The great batlike rays with venomous barbs and wingspreads of four or five feet and weighing several hundred pounds are usually found sleeping in the sand. They are so sluggish that you can often touch them before they take off with a rush and graceful flapping of wings. Spearing a sleeping ray is no challenge, but some divers will occasionally take a big one for the tremendous fight they put up. The only danger is being struck by the poison barb or stinger which causes such excruciating pain that it has been known to paralyze a full-grown man. When speared in the middle of the back, the pull of the line sometimes causes the ray to turn upside down and swoop back at the diver. Aim at the head so there is less chance of an accidental encounter with its vicious barb. A hand spear with a short cable on the detachable head is even safer, and you have the extra thrill of trying to hang on to a fighting ray at close quarters.

Manta rays, or devilfish, are real behemoths of the sea with powerful, batlike wings that measure over 20 feet from tip to tip, and bodies that weigh as much as 4000 pounds. This legendary creature is called devilfish because of two powerful, muscular arms on each side of its head that are used to sweep plankton, shrimp and small fish into its cavernous mouth. Unlike other rays, mantas do not sleep and feed on the bottom, but cruise the open sea in search of free-floating or free-swimming food. Often they can be seen leaping out of the water, their tremendous bodies erupting in a shower of spray and sailing through the air like some giant, prehistoric bird. Usually they turn upside down and fall backward to the surface, crashing into the water with a prodigious splash that can be heard for miles. Legends tagged the manta with a fearful reputation and fishermen love to tell stories of devilfish flying out of the water in deliberate attacks on boats. Actually they are harmless, docile creatures and the only danger to skin divers is that one might make a flying leap and accidentally come down on top of their head. They do not have a barb or stinger in their tail to be afraid of and cruise so slowly, that a diver can swim right alongside, close enough to touch them with his hands. They are too big to spear with anything less than a hawser strong enough to tow a boat. And you had best be aboard the boat or have a second means of transportation, because mantas harpooned from the surface have been known to tow a 36-foot boat for hours. But their docility and huge size has tempted some of us to try a short-lived, barehanded manta ride.

I tried my first manta ride while diving with Raul Echeverria off Puerta Vallarta, Mexico. A friend had described Tom Hubbel's technique of manta riding off Grand Cayman island, and I was eager to find out what it was like. We were free diving off a point near Yalapa, and mantas were coming by every few minutes as regularly as streetcars. The water was full of plankton, limiting visibility to about 25 feet, which didn't give us much time to maneuver into position. A great black shadow appeared out of the mist, its tremendous bat-like wings spread wide, it sailed slowly through the water about 20 feet below. I dived on an interception course and the manta changed direction, coming up to meet me head on. I hung motionless, looking into an open mouth that appeared as wide as a truck bed. The short arms, or flippers, on each side were extended as if ready to sweep me into its maw. The white of its underbelly extended out beneath wings that had a spread of at least 16 feet. I had the feeling of being tied to a railroad track and watching a freight train approach. About six feet away, the manta dived, flapped its wings, and was gone before I recovered from the shock of that open mouth.

The next one performed according to the book and stayed on course. I swam over its back between the immense wings, reached forward with my gloved hands, and grabbed the top edge of its open mouth, near the sides. I felt a tremendous surge as the manta leaped forward. Water roared past my ears, tore at my mask and almost broke my grip. The strain was terrific, my arms ached and with each stroke of those mighty wings, the speed increased. I felt the beast dive, my ears popped with the pressure. Then we went roaring toward the surface, shooting vertically straight up. I had visions of hurtling through the air on the monster's back and being crushed beneath tons of devilfish as it crashed backward into the water. I let go and peeled off, feeling its sandpaper skin scrape my elbows and thigh as it zoomed past. I stayed submerged, waiting until I heard the reverberating crash at the end of its aerial flight. The entire ride lasted only a few seconds, but it was one of the most exhilarating few seconds I have ever experienced. However, I doubt that manta riding will ever become popular. These monsters are so big and so powerful that, as the Mexican boatman said, "A guy could get hurt doing that."

The sea-going mammals, seals, sea lions, porpoises and whales, should never be speared. Not only because they are friendly, warm-blooded creatures usually protected by law, but they are intelligent and their reactions would be entirely different from that of lower forms of life. Sharks, fish, rays and eels instinctively fight the spear that impales them, and it is a rare accident when they turn on the diver. But a seal or porpoise is intelligent enough to know immediately where the spear came from and would give the diver a very bad time. None of these animals are a danger to a diver if left unmolested.

Even the orca, or dreaded killer whale, the scourge of the seas that slaughters seals and porpoises for the pleasure of killing, has now been shown to be tolerant of, and even friendly, to divers. A number of encounters with killer whales in various parts of the world, in which the skin divers came off scot free, placed doubts as to the danger of these animals to humans. Then Namu, a bull orca, was captured and placed in a fenced-off section of Puget Sound, where divers discovered they could swim and play with him in the water as if he were a giant pet. Now, Gary Keffler, a skin diver who owns Underwater Sports Dive Shop in Seattle, has a regular job of untangling captured, wild killers from the nets, and Gary has not yet been attacked. The first attack by a killer whale on a skin diver has yet to be recorded.

Porpoises are notoriously friendly to man, and are so intelligent that most of their trainers and many scientists believe their brain is superior to ours. As Rico Browning, who trains Flipper for the TV series, said, "The problem isn't in Flipper learning a new trick, it's just that I'm too dumb to let him know what I want him to do. Sometimes he seems to figure out what I want before I decide how I'm going to tell him." Porpoises have a complicated system of communication by a series of clicks, whistles and beeps, which scientists believe is a sophisticated language. If we can decipher this language and learn

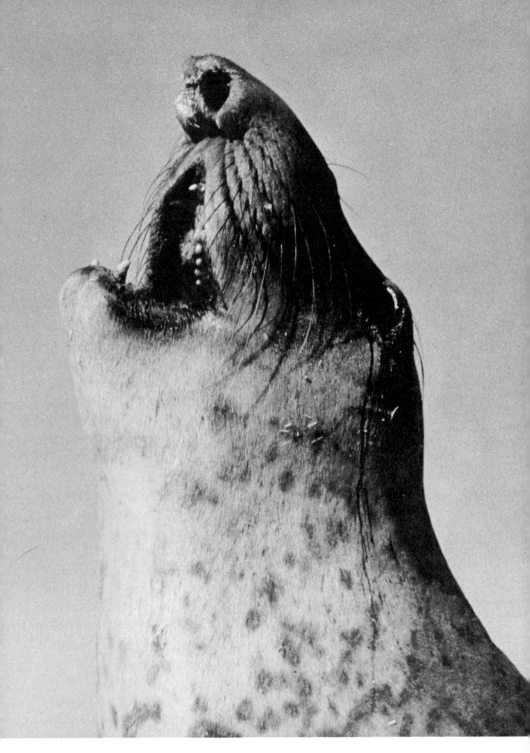

Seals, sea lions, porpoise and other mammals should never be speared. This young male elephant seal is trumpeting to scare off intruders and protect his harem. (*Photo by Mick Church*)

to communicate with porpoises, our knowledge of the sea would increase fantastically, and we would have a valuable ally. Porpoises navigate by bouncing echoes off objects in the water, and their sonar is so refined that even while blindfolded they can detect the difference between an artificial fish and a real one. Killer whales have the same facility of "seeing" with their entire head, so a skin diver who thinks he is hidden from a killer by remaining quiet is only kidding himself.

The California sea lions, so often seen performing in circuses and vaudeville acts, balancing balls on their noses and clapping their flippers in applause of their own performances, seem to be delighted when skin divers join them in the water. The small ones love to show off for the clumsy divers, performing spectacular aquabatics at dazzling speeds. They are more graceful than a ballet dancer and have perfect control, even at high speeds. Traveling at high speed, they can throw out their flippers and turn or stop as suddenly as if they hit a wall. This ability can be unnerving to the uninitiated when some of the females start playing a game of "who can come closest to the diver without hitting him?" Many times I have hung helpless in the water and watched a sea lion streaking like a torpedo directly at my head and braced myself for the impact, only to have it throw on the brakes and stop, inches away, with its eye peering into my mask. But, as with all animal life, a diver will occasionally run into a grouchy old bull who has been driven away from his herd of females by a younger male, and he is in no mood to be tampered with. Any time you are challenged by a big bull sea lion, the judicious course to follow is to get out of the water.

As we stated in Chapter 1, the popular concept of the submarine world as a place inhabited by vicious sea monsters waiting to attack a hapless diver is pure nonsense. This is an old wives' tale, which the face mask, spear gun and camera of the underwater hunter has thoroughly debunked. Man is the aggressor underwater as he is on land, and as the jungle hunter has more to fear from insects and swamps than from lions and tigers, the underwater hunter has more to fear from sea urchins and currents than from sharks and barracuda. However, in the ocean as in the jungles, only the foolhardy plunges in without adequate training, equipment and preparation. Always keep in mind that, when underwater, what you don't know *can* hurt you.

The California sea lions, so often seen performing in vaudeville acts, seem to be delighted when skin divers join them in the water. (*Photo by Chuck Nicklin*)

Give Americans a stick and a ball, and in ten minutes they will have a game going. With enough time they will promote the game into regional, national and international competitions. (*Photo courtesy of Robert Lee Studio*)

12   *Competition Divers*

GIVE Americans a stick and a ball, and in ten minutes they will have a game going. Given enough time they will promote the game into regional, national and international competitions for the championship of the world. Americans are probably the world's most competitive sportsmen, and skin divers are no exception. Unlike spectator sports where competitors perform for the benefit of large audiences, a skin diver competes beneath the surface, unseen and unapplauded by anyone except possibly his diving buddy. No accolade or praise is received for a valiant effort or a brilliant play, and results are appreciated only by other competitors. Yet the desire for recognition is so strong that men and women drive themselves to unbelievable feats of stamina and endurance to determine "who is best" in one of the world's most grueling contests.

A true spearfishing champion learns to spend most of his time on the bottom, at depths ranging from fifty to one hundred feet, and he holds his breath all the time he is under. But diving deep and often is only a small part of the requirements. The champion must recognize his fish instantly so he doesn't waste time on unwanted species. He must also learn to judge the size of his quarry with equal speed, or he again wastes valuable time. All this is accomplished while holding his breath, often in water with visibility less than the length of his spear gun. He learns to judge the current, the surge and the kelp, and make them work in his favor rather than against him. He studies the bottom terrain, and can detect holes and caves occupied by fish instead of empty water. The champion is as much at home under water as most people are in an automobile, diving gear is as familiar to him as a pair of shoes and he can find fish in any kind of weather and any kind of water.

But above all else, the champion spearfisherman is an amazing specimen of physical stamina and endurance. Others may swim faster, dive deeper and in some cases even stay underwater longer. But what other sport requires a man to be clearheaded, alert and well co-ordinated after four hours of continuous diving to depths between fifty and one hundred feet? The big one may not show up until near the end of such grueling effort. When this happens, the champion will hit it, ride out its underwater run, and fight it to the surface while still holding his breath. And he will have enough steam left to make the staging area before the final gun goes off.

In other words, the spearfishing champion must develop the swimming ability of a seal, the stamina of a grizzly bear, the sea lore of an oceanographer, the fish knowledge of a marine biologist, the bottom knowledge of a marine geologist and the watermanship of a South Seas pearl diver. His hunting accuracy is a combination of the skills of Robin Hood and Daniel Boone and, to land his catch, he often must combine the methods of an underwater cowboy with the finesse of an accomplished marlin fisherman.

National and international competitions in the United States are sanctioned by the Amateur Athletic Union (AAU), and are governed and administered by the Underwater Society of America, which represents the diving clubs through their regional councils or associations. The Society has a vice-president in charge of scuba competitions, and a vice-president in charge of skin-diving competitions, but the real authority and incentive is vested in the regional councils, which represent the more than 1000 individual diving clubs scattered across America. Competitions among the clubs and councils include formal scuba decathlons, underwater hockey, treasure hunts and scavenger hunts, but by far the most popular and the most hotly contested, on a national scale, are the spearfishing contests, especially those for free diving without the use of scuba. Competitive spearfishermen are the "purists" of skin diving, who disdain the use of scuba as a crutch unworthy of a true sportsman. They delight in their ability to stalk fish at great depths while holding their breath, and they subject themselves to rigorous training to develop skill and physical perfection. But their most outstanding characteristic is the lengths to which they will go in order to win a contest or a meet. This competi-

The rivalry between clubs made interclub competitions inevitable, and spearfishing contests are now an important segment of organized diving. (*Photo by Paul Tzimoulis*)

tive spirit became apparent with the formation of the first diving clubs in the 1930s and '40s, before scuba became available.

Competitive-minded divers of early clubs set themselves apart from the average by establishing special categories and awards which recognized unusual feats and exceptional prowess. An example was the Inglewood, California Sharks Club, which required a diver to grab a three-foot angel shark by the tail and wrestle it to shore barehanded before he could become a full-fledged member. One enthusiastic candidate grabbed a shark that was too big to handle. The shark grabbed the front of the diver's swim trunks in its mouth, missing meat by inches. Unlike most sharks which rip and slash, the angel hangs on like a bulldog, and the hapless diver found himself trying to hold off a four-foot shark that was latched to his trunks with a grip of death. The diver's buddy tried to help, but couldn't pull the shark loose and each time the victim relaxed his grip the shark gained a little more swim suit and came a little closer to vital organs. The situation was saved in the nick of time by the judicious use of a diver's knife to cut away the swim trunks. The club membership committee ruled that catching a shark with your swim trunks was illegal and the diver was forced to try again before he could join the club.

Other clubs established more difficult and more stringent feats to show the superiority of their members. Typical of these was the "King Neptune" award set up by my club, the Los Angeles Neptunes. In order to wear the badge of a King Neptune, a member had to perform the following feats while holding his breath: Catch a two-foot shark barehanded; find, pry off and bring up, three abalone in a single dive; catch two legal lobsters in one dive; and spear four different species of fish in a single day, with at least one fish weighing over fifteen pounds. The San Diego Bottom Scratchers, the world's first skin-diving club, formed in 1933, had similar requirements but demanded that their members perform all of the feats on the same day.

This rivalry between clubs made an interclub contest inevitable, and the first formal underwater spearfishing competition was held in 1949 between the Los Angeles Neptunes and the Southern California Skin Divers Association. It was agreed that each club would enter a six-man team. The rules were loose and anything we could spear legally would be counted, including sharks, rays, eels, even a whale if

National championships at Newport, Rhode Island, 1961. Connecticut girl's team took first place in the women's division. (*Photo by Paul Tzimoulis*)

we could land one. Our club held a strategy meeting and agreed that a big shark would probably win, so we decided to take advantage of the fact that sharks are attracted by blood in the water. On the day of the contest, we purchased a gallon jug of beef blood from a butcher shop and took it out into the water with us.

It was a cold, rainy winter day, when twelve of us packed our gear down the cliff at Flat Rock Point, Palos Verdes and prepared to enter our first contest. A huge surf was running and as I rode my float out through the breakers, I almost lost our jug of shark bait. Beyond the breakers, the water was clear enough to see the bottom, and my team-mates raced ahead looking for a good place to plant our bloody bait. The bottom was a jagged mass of solid rock, covered by a jungle of kelp and seaweed. We found a small, sandy clearing in thirty feet of water and planted our blood next to a crevice leading out to deep water. I pulled the cork, and we spent the next hour lying on the surface watching the blood ooze slowly from the jug and dissipate into the blue water. Not a single shark appeared, and finally one of our teammates commented that while we were wasting time waiting for a shark, the other team was busy winning the contest. Disgusted, I smashed the jug with a rock, and our team belatedly began some serious underwater hunting. Fifteen minutes before the end of the meet, we bumped into a leopard shark sleeping peacefully under a ledge not more than 20 feet from our jug of blood. Its weight tipped the scales enough in our favor to win the contest. But, to this day, the opposing team is convinced that we won by foul means, so the victory had a hollow satisfaction.

Modern spearfishing competitions are a far cry from that crude beginning, and the rivalry is even more keen. Elaborate rules have been

The race to be the first team on a reef causes a mad scramble at the sound of the starting gun. (*Photo courtesy of* Skin Diver *magazine*)

established by the competitive committee of the regional Councils of Diving Clubs, and are enforced by monitors while divers are in the water. Only certain species of fish in an area are permitted, size limits are established, and points awarded according to the rarity of the species or the difficulty in spearing and landing it. A contestant who happens to luck into a single giant jewfish or large grouper may still lose the contest on points.

Individual clubs enter three-man teams in local elimination contests and the winners of these compete to determine the national champions. This team then represents the United States in world competitions with teams from other countries. Contests last for a period of four to five hours, and may be held in waters ranging from the cold, turbulent northeast coast of Maine, through the powerful surge and heavy kelp of Southern California, to the warm, clear waters of the Caribbean. The divers sometimes work from boats, but more often from a staging area on shore. Boundaries of the contest area are announced well in advance, and scouting is permitted several weeks before the day of the competition.

Championships are often won or lost by the thoroughness with which a team scouts an area. This is the time that visiting skin divers become acquainted with the terrain, learn to recognize the local species of fish, discover their habits and find the best spots to hunt. Teams have devised ingenious methods of marking hot spots, fish holes and ledges without tipping off the location to other divers. Cross bearings from shore are not dependable if a fog closes in on the day of the meet. Some divers mount a compass on their paddleboard and count the number of strokes, or time their travel, to a fish hole. Others anchor an innocent-appearing piece of driftwood, coconut shell or seaweed over the holes. And, to frustrate teams spying on them from shore, false markers are often sprinkled over barren bottom which cause a "spy" team to waste valuable time and let the scouting team get to the fish first. The race to be the first team on a reef causes a mad scramble at the starting gun. Oars are not permitted on floats used at shore-based meets, and special competition paddleboards have been developed which will let a spearfisherman move over the water surface rapidly while carrying 200 pounds of fish and equipment in addition to the diver. No spear guns are permitted which do not utilize a diver's own muscles to cock, so CO_2 and gas guns are illegal.

Hunting fish underwater requires a high degree of skill and ability under any circumstances, and when practiced in competition with top experts, the skills and techniques are drawn to a fine degree of perfection. An appreciation of the fish knowledge and fish sense accumulated by a champion spearfisherman is revealed in a letter received from Terry Maas, of the San Jose Skin Diver's Club, who is the 1968 National Individual Champion, and a member of the three-man team that won the National Championships at Carmel, California.

Terry is talking about the habits of ling cod, the prize fish of central and Northern California divers. He says, "Lings are found at all depths from five to eighty feet and deeper, on rocky bottoms only. A good place to look for them is beneath a school of any size of blue rockfish. "Blues" are their favorite food. About half of the lings live in very characteristic holes, which are in the shape of long, horizontal cracks with openings no more than six inches to 1½ feet high. Very big rocky holes rarely hold lings. It is the smaller holes, just big enough for the fish, that are preferred. Lings spend about half of their day out sitting on top of rocks. If you see several out, you can expect to find most all of the lings out for the next several hours. Likewise, if the only place they are seen is in holes, then don't spend time looking for them in the open. They are often found lying on the tops and sides of pinnacles arising from deep water. When found in a hole, if they make no attempt to escape, they can usually be expected to stay in that hole. I have returned to crevices years later and recognized the same fish by the scars on its head. It is for this reason that we spend many hours hunting for these cave fish, because, on the day of the contest, we can find the fish in its hole 50 per cent of the time.

"A tip on hunting lings is that if you are skimming the bottom and flush a ling that swims away slowly, you can almost always get him. If he bolts, you are out of luck, so if he lazily swims away, don't follow or he will bolt. The trick is to stop dead still and sink to the bottom. The curious ling will almost always return from the same direction, and will swim right up to your outstretched gun.

"A five-prong spearhead is best for lings up to 30 pounds. A good place to shoot is vertically, just behind the gill plates. If the fish is facing you in a hole, just turn the prongs horizontally and aim at a level slightly above the eyes. This usually stones them. Before I learned this trick, many big lings tore off my shaft.

"Almost all of the fish in Northern California are found in holes on dirty days. The only time I don't carry a light is when I'm strictly hunting free-swimming fish. Lights are carried in the left hand and a neoprene strap connects them to the wrist so we can let them go when we string a fish. Lights mounted on guns are no good, because you can cover more of the inside of a hole without the long lever caused by the gun. When you survey a hole with a light and spot a fish, shut off the light until your gun is in position, then flick it on and shoot. A light on a fish for the time it takes to position your gun is often just enough to spook the fish.

"I'm strictly against the use of reels on fish under 50 pounds. The

Fish brought to shore during a competition are tabulated by Fish and Game officials according to size, specie and number, weighed by a judge, and then turned over to an orphanage or hospital. (*Photo by Paul Tzimoulis*)

Getting to the fish first is so important that special, competition-type paddle-boards have been developed. (*Photo courtesy of* Skin Diver *magazine*)

reels are too bulky and when you do "pop" your reel and head for the surface, the fish below is spending all of his time seeing how tangled he can become. The best policy is to use a short line, and when you shoot a fish, pull him out as quickly as you can while he is still stunned from the shock of the hit."

Terry landed two big lings during the 1968 National Competitions, both of which he had spotted at least eight times previously, and they were in the same holes on the day of the meet.

H. Gene Martin, another national champion, who lives in Portland, Oregon, and is a member of the Oregon Sea Lions Diving Club, also gives us an indication of the fish lore these competition divers accumulate. Gene's prize fish are also ling cod and cabezon, so we have a comparison of knowledge and techniques between two top-notch spearfishermen.

Gene says, "Anyone who calls himself a spearfisherman in Oregon is also a free diver. Our diving is in bays and on offshore reefs, seldom past fifty feet. We would use tanks if we thought it would help, but under our conditions, it doesn't. We use competition-type paddleboards exclusively, no boats at all, and we make extensive use of fathometers to locate offshore reefs and pinnacles. Our guns are all rubber powered, of a type that can be easily modified to our purposes. We normally remove the safety; make new stainless shafts, as the chrome-plated shafts tend to chip and rust; make our own rubber bands, usually of $\frac{5}{8}$- or $\frac{9}{16}$-inch-diameter tubing; cut out the muzzle, and install rubber retainers so the bands will not flip over the end of the gun and be out of position when it is loaded again. It is important to cut out the muzzle, as a big cabezon will snap it in two if the shaft is not all the way out of the gun.

"Our visibility ranges from two feet to thirty feet, with an average of eight feet. The visibility is best in spring and fall, and the weather is too rough for any diving between November and March.

"The ling cod is a bottom fish that prefers an uneven, rocky area with lots of hiding places. The female is the largest of the species, growing as big as ninety pounds. The male seldom exceeds thirty pounds. The female spawns in late winter and early spring, and after she has deposited her mass of white, tapicoca-like eggs, she heads back for deep water to recuperate. The smaller and more aggressive

You don't have to be a champion, or engage in competitive events to enjoy spearfishing. But you can learn more in three months with a competitive club than in three years on your own. (*Photo courtesy of* Skin Diver *magazine*)

male stays and guards her eggs until they are hatched. We make it a practice not to hunt the male guarders during the time they are on the eggs because they will not leave the area and are easy to shoot. As soon as the male guarder is shot, perch and starfish eat the eggs. Lings like deep water and the bigger ones are usually found below thirty feet, past the vegetation line. We try to hit them directly behind the head, because it usually kills them and the shaft is easier to extract from this boneless area.

"The cabezon is the easiest fish to shoot that we have, but he is also the most difficult to find. This is because of his protective coloration. He likes rocky areas with some short kelp growing on it to hide him. The cabezon feeds mainly on crabs and prefers to live on a granite-reef area that is surrounded by sand, thus providing protection and food supply close by. Cabs are usually shallow-living fish, found between 3 feet and 40 feet. Eighty per cent of them in our waters are taken above 15 feet. Spotting a cab is difficult because they are shaped much like the rocks they lie on, and are able to change their color at will. The normal colors are green, gray, brown and yellow. Sometimes you will see one that is almost pure white. These are the less intelligent ones, and they don't last long when spearfishermen are in the area. The cabezon depends on his coloration to a ridiculous degree, as you can normally touch them with your hand before they will take off. It is important to shoot them while they are sitting still, as they are one of the fastest fish I have ever seen for short distances. They know only one speed—full ahead. We try not to shoot them directly in the head as their head is very bony and it is difficult to get a five tine out of it. We try to shoot them from directly above, with the five tine landing at right angles to the backbone, so the shot will kill.

"The black rockfish is a free-swimming school fish. A big one in our area is anything over 4 pounds. We find these fish in kelp beds between 5 feet and 60 feet. They are a very wary fish, and so require some careful stalking. The best way to hunt them is to locate the school and then begin the dive about 20 feet away so that they can be approached on the bottom. Diving directly down into blacks will only cause them to scatter and hole up. When the school comes into view, you need only to lie still and pick out the biggest one, then move easily toward him until you are in range. These fish we also shoot just behind the gills with the five tine striking vertically on the side of the fish. In dirty water, the rockfish is one of the few fish we can spear, as we can get on the bottom and look up to silhouette them against the light."

As in all other sports, you don't have to be a champion or engage in competitive events to enjoy spearfishing, but they set the pace, and you can improve your techniques, sharpen your skills and increase your enjoyment by following their example. You can learn more about spearfishing in three months with a competitive diving club than you can in three years on your own.

Bibliography

Skin Diving Books

BARADA, BILL. *Underwater*. California: Peterson Publishing Company, 1954.

————*Adventure Underwater*. California: Peterson Publishing Company, 1959.

————*Let's Go Diving*. California: U. S. Divers Company, 1962. (This booklet is a condensed instruction manual used extensively by instructors throughout America and Mexico.)

BRIDGES, LLOYD, as told to BILL BARADA. *Mask and Flippers*. Pennsylvania: Chilton Publishing Company, 1960. (In the words of Mike Nelson, the hero of television's "Sea Hunt," tells the story of skin diving and how safety rules were learned, the hard way.)

CONFERENCE FOR NATIONAL COOPERATION IN AQUATICS. *New Science of Skin and Scuba Diving*. New York: Association Press, 1962, revised regularly.

COUSTEAU, J. Y., and FRÉDÉRIC DUMAS. *The Silent World*. New York: Harper Publishing Company, 1953. (On the best seller list, made into a motion picture.)

LEE, O. *The Complete Illustrated Guide To Snorkel and Deep Diving.* New York: Doubleday & Company, 1963.

————*The Skin Diver's Manual.* New York: Doubleday & Company, 1968.

TILLMAN, ALBERT. *Underwater Education.* Iowa: William Brown and Company, 1962. (Al Tillman was president of the National Association of Underwater Instructors (NAUI) for many years.)

UNITED STATES NAVY DIVING MANUAL. *NAVSHIPS 250–538.* Superintendent of Documents, U. S. Government Printing Office, Washington, D. C. (Official manual of U. S. Navy.)

Books About the Sea and Fish

CARSON, RACHEL. *The Sea Around Us.* New York: Oxford Press, 1951. (A best seller made into a motion picture.)

DUGAN, JAMES, ROBERT COWAN, BILL BARADA, LUIS MARDEN, and RICHARD CRUM. *World Beneath The Sea.* Washington D.C.: National Geographic Society, 1967. (Excellent illustrations and text.)

HALSTEAD, B. W. (M.D.) *Dangerous Marine Animals.* Maryland: Cornell Maritime Press, 1959.

NATIONAL GEOGRAPHIC SOCIETY STAFF. *Wondrous World of Fishes.* Washington D.C., 1965.

RAY, DR. C., and E. CIAMPI. *The Underwater Guide To Marine Life.* New York: A. S. Barnes Company, 1956.

ZIM, DR. H. S., and DR. H. H. SHOEMAKER. *Fishes.* New York: Simon and Schuster, 1956.

Shell Books

ABBOTT, R. TUCKER. *American Sea Shells.* New Jersey: Van Nostrand, 1967, revised.

HOYT, MURRAY. *Jewels From the Ocean Deep.* New York: G. P. Putnam's Sons, 1967.

MORRIS, PERCY A. *Field Guide To The Shells.* Boston: Houghton Mifflin Company, 1953 (Two books) *Atlantic and Gulf Coasts,* and *Pacific Coast and Hawaii,* including Gulf of California, Mexico.

TINKER, SPENCER W. *Pacific Sea Shells.* Vermont: Charles Tuttle Company, 1957. (Tinker is Director of Aquarium, University of Hawaii.)

Underwater Photography Books

CROSS, E. R. *Underwater Photography and Television.* New York: Exposition Press, 1954.

REBIKOFF, D. and P. CHERNEY. *A Guide To Underwater Photography.* New York: Greenberg, 1955.

SCHENCK, H., JR., and H. KENDALL. *Underwater Photography.* Maryland: Cornell Maritime Press, 1954.

STARK, DR. W. A. II, and P. BRUNDZA. *The Art of Underwater Photography.* New York: Chilton, 1966. (Dr. Stark's photos and work appear frequently in *National Geographic* and other media. Paul Brundza owns a film-processing company in Marathon, Florida.)

TZIMOULIS, P. and H. FRY. *Camera Below.* New York: Association Press, 1968. (Paul Tzimoulis is editor and publisher of *Skin Diver* magazine.)

Index